In the Blink of an Eye
The Journey from Grief to Hope

by Gwen Lavender

In the Blink of an Eye: The Journey from Grief to Hope

By Gwen Lavender

Copyright © 2024 by Gwen Lavender

All rights reserved. No part of this book may be reproduced, stored in a retrieval system, or transmitted in any form or by any means, electronic, mechanical, photocopying, recording, or otherwise, without the prior written permission of the publisher or author, except for the use of brief quotations in a book review.

ISBN: 979-8-9914376-7-7

Printed in the USA

Edited by Neha Sinha
Cover design and illustrations by Chahat Bassi

Tribute

To my Late husband, McArthur Lavender. I am blessed to have had you as my husband for 43 years and 10 months. I love you dearly.

Your legacy – sons Troy, Jason, and Chris; daughter, Ginger; and your grandchildren and their children's children – will carry you with them.

You will always live in our hearts.

Acknowledgments

Most of all, I thank my Heavenly Father who has kept me through it all and for calling me to share my story.

Thank you to my Faith, Family, Friends, and the many divine connections who supported and prayed for me. God sent you to encourage me, wipe my tears, and wrap your arms around me when I needed it most.

Thank you to the angels that God introduced me to for the first time during my grief season – Donna, Janet, Angel, Linda and Neha. Thank you to my teachers past and present. To Minister Janice, Coach Kim Horvath, Dr. Ginger Lavender Wilkerson, Dr. Sandra Hardy and my Pastor, Dr. Kimberlyn J. Jones, who saw in me what I could not see in myself.

All of you have helped me to walk again, to put one foot in front of the other, and move forward through the darkest days of my grief journey.

Foreword

"In the Blink of an Eye" is a heartfelt memoir in which Gwen stops and reflects on the 43-year, 10-month span of her life that she shared with her beloved husband McArthur, lovingly nicknamed Mac and PeeWee.

Mother to mother, sister to sister, friend to friend, brother to brother, her sage advice and compelling story offer us a rare opportunity to see what deep love and deep loss look like.

In the process she challenges everyone, no matter what stage of life you are in, to ask the hard questions that will help you through the long nights and difficult days that often accompany the work of grieving the loss of a loved one, or two or three. In the blink of an eye, 2020 showed up at her door.

Death, and the accompanying grief, did not ask her permission to visit, nor did it follow any logical prescriptive plan as to who, what, why, or when it would be her turn. It just showed up and changed her life forever.

In this book, Gwen, graciously and unselfishly shares what it has been like for her, and being the truth-teller that she is, she opens up to others so that they will not have to "suffer in silence", nor scramble to find resources as they adjust to the reality of their new normal. She reminds us that God is always with us, that his love is more than enough to carry us through, and that with this assurance, we will survive and thrive again. But, we will have to go through it.

Finally, Gwen is a master builder of friendships, family, and community. Although the community still has room to grow, through it all, she has found a renewed commitment to loving and sharing with others as crucial to her ongoing healing and helping journey.

Gwen states in her own words: "My destiny is to keep on living, to speak and minister as an ambassador for Christ, using my personal life experiences as testimony of the goodness of God through it all."

We are not spared the pain of loss because we are believers. Grief is real and must be paid its due. However, as Gwen demonstrates over and over again – life keeps calling and we find the strength to do what must be done. We are more than conquerors, and God is no stranger to death; he continues to have the last victory over the valleys of death and all the shadows that would reside there.

– Dr. Sandra Hardy

Table of Contents

Acknowledgments i

Foreword ii

Chapter 1 – Going Through 1

Chapter 2 – Seasons of Change 12

Chapter 3 – In the Blink of an Eye 26

Chapter 4 – The Toughest Decision of My Life 37

Chapter 5 – A Farewell With Love 54

Chapter 6 – Whispers In The Night 68

Chapter 7 – Strength In The Storm 78

Chapter 8 – Divinely Connected Community 88

Chapter 9 – Dancing With Memories 108

Chapter 10 – Choosing Life: Embracing The New Normal... 116

Epilogue 126

Appendix A – Paying It Forward 129

Appendix B – Scriptures 130

Appendix C – Definitions 136

About Gwen 139

Hope is the Thing with Feathers

by Emily Dickinson

Hope is the thing with feathers
That perches in the soul,
And sings the tune without the words,
And never stops at all,

And sweetest in the gale is heard;
And sore must be the storm
That could abash the little bird
That kept so many warm.

I've heard it in the chillest land,
And on the strangest sea;
Yet, never, in extremity,
It asked a crumb of me.

Chapter 1

Going Through

"The oak fought the wind and was broken, the willow bent when it must and survived."

— Robert Jordan

The Cleveland Clinic reports that the average person blinks 14 to 17 times a minute. That comes out to 840 to 1,020 blinks every hour. If you sleep for 8 hours every night, you blink about 13,440 to 16,320 times a day.

Take a moment right now and notice the blinking of your eyes. In the Blink of an Eye, life as we know it can change or leave just like that.

Doing this exercise helps us realize how fragile life is, and the importance of not taking things, even the things we may consider small, for granted.

When I took the first step down this foggy winding road, to sit in the seat where many widows sat before me, I saw myself living two different stories at the same time. My "outside story" and my "inside story".

My initial outside story was that of shock and denial. It didn't seem real. I silently screamed at the top of my lungs, "Help me! Help me! I can't do this. Give me more time! What can I do to stop it? This can't be happening."

I felt alone in a place where I had never been before. It was a fearful, painful, surreal reality to see my husband unresponsive. The possibility that he was dying, to think that we would be separated and that I would be alone was inconceivable. What am I to do? On one hand, I wanted to retreat, crawl into a corner, cover my head, and wait until it was over, until I woke up from this nightmare.

But my inside story was, in essence, a quiet voice within that assured me to say out loud to myself, "I'm going to get through this, although I don't know how, and I don't know when". I knew I had to lean in and deal with reality of what was before me; and go with the process as it unfolded, to get to the other side.

Inside, I was clothed with a blessed confidence that I would get to the other side. I tried my hardest to trust that my next breath would take me to my next step.

And it did.

* * *

When I am "going through", I think of my migraines, the debilitating headaches that I experience from time to time. I use it as my measuring tool, my reassuring proof of the facts, and the anchor for my hope of making it to the other side. God has provided me with a vivid and colorful firsthand illustration of what going through looks like, feels like, smells like, sounds like, and tastes like. Migraines are a bitter pill, it's the "thorn in my side" and the "barbed wires in my eyes".

Migraines are one of the first things I experienced that had the power to stop me in my tracks in the blink of an eye. Since then, I have had more experiences that had the same powerful effect, including the recurring waves of grief in the loss of a loved one.

Grief heartaches and migraine headaches clearly speak to my body and soul, demanding my attention, "Hold up, wait a minute, you ain't going nowhere. Sit down, lay down, slow down, chill out. Be still, and go through the process. You can't avoid me. You can't rush me. Recognize and respect who I am. It is something that I have no control over, yet before it overtakes me, I can see signs of it's coming. I prepare and brace myself for the journey from one side to the other. I am fully aware and know that no one could go through the process for me. It is a solo experience.

However, I am not doing this by myself. I am not alone. I have support waiting outside the door of my being, to help me in any way they can. They just can't get to the inside and go through the experience with me. I recall saying to Mac, "Oh, no, I'm getting a migraine. I'm going to lay down," he would say, "Okay," and go downstairs. After a while, he would tiptoe to the door, whispering "Are you okay" and I would reply, "I will be shortly. It's a process."

He was there to support me, although he could only go so far to help me, checking on me from time to time, seeing if there was something I needed and if I was okay. And I missed that dearly. This type of thing, you may take for granted but it is huge when you don't have it.

As the migraine takes over and the inside process begins, there is no turning around. I have an assurance that I am connected to God and that He is guiding me to the other side. I steady myself and lean into what I recall and know from past experiences, about my God and the connections who are waiting for me. I hold the vision, trust the process, and ride the waves to the other side.

I call this *Going Through*.

No matter what my plan is for the day, work or play, home or away, with others or alone; there is the real possibility that a migraine will show up. It's the quiet before the storm, warning that it will soon hit.

I am acquainted with specific things that trigger my migraines – certain foods, fluorescent lights, perfumes, and stress, among others. I get an early warning sign one or two days ahead of the actual headache: food cravings, stiff neck, mood changes, and, oddly enough, I yawn a lot. I feel off balance in some way, but keep going and going, and doing and doing. With this window of opportunity to prepare and brace myself, I carry a migraine kit with me. Like any pending storm, I always have a choice to pay close attention and take some preventive measures or to ignore them and suffer the migraine. But either way, within days, the headache will come.

So it is with the heartache of grief.

* * *

Here's what happens on a typical migraine day.

I can see it coming, like a freight train with bold red flags waving warnings. I say to myself, "Oh no", "why", and "not now" and with a feeling of disappointment, I rush to stop whatever I am doing and go with the flow of the process. Within minutes, I am stopped in my tracks and have to find a place to be still and close my eyes. Can I beat the traffic and get home before the onset? If I am in the comfort of my home I will lie down, and cover my head. At work, I will close my office door and put my head on my desk. If I'm driving, I pull over, park the car, and lay my head back. At church, I will leave the crowd. I grasp my purse and leave the sanctuary quickly to sit in a dark classroom. If with a friend, I tell them what to expect as I nervously dig in my purse for my dark sunglasses. I tell them that I'm having a migraine, that I will close my eyes and rest in the quiet for a little while and I will be okay.

Once, my husband and I had an early morning flight. I had very little sleep the night before. We made it to the airport a couple of hours early and finished checking in. As soon as I sat down, I felt a migraine coming on. I braced myself and went through the process. We boarded the plane and I went to sleep. I am so thankful that Peewee was right there next to me.

When it suddenly comes knocking at my door, I must answer. With my eyes closed, I feel the familiar tingles, pins-and-needles sensations in my hands and feet. The familiar visual auras start as small squiggles embedded in my eye that gradually expand to a lightning bolt in one eye and build up to blind spots. Then, the final manifestation into a colorful 4th of July fireworks show within my head. In my mind's eye, it's like a kaleidoscope, with constantly changing patterns and colors. The entire cycle ranges from 30-35 minutes. Each time, I hope, pray, believe, and expect this one to follow the pattern of my previous migraines and each one has, without exception. Once the visual auras are gone, I open one eye and peek at the clock on the nightstand next to my bed; it is ticking loudly, trying not to rush movement so I wait quietly a little longer. If I move quickly, or start stirring too soon, it could trigger another migraine and back-to-back migraines are to be avoided at all costs.

Although this phase of the migraine is over, my strength and energy are drained. I am sensitive to light, sound, smell, and touch. I grab my dark sunglasses, to shield the glare of all light. Dark sunglasses are my best friends for the next 24 hours. Yes, I can function, but I would rather retreat, sleep and disconnect from interacting with others.

There is a TV commercial about migraines that best describes how I feel for the next 48 hours as I push myself to go from place to place, "I show up, but migraines prevent me from saying I am here".

Migraines, like grief surges, are recurring. Although I have been through migraines a hundred times, and unimaginable surges and seasons of grief over the past 4 years, it does not make the next encounter easier. Each experience is uniquely its own.

I have found that just like most things in life, it is a process.

As I reflect on the similarities between the migraines and my grief, I know that it's my faith (belief, confidence, trust) in God and His Word that sustains and assures me that I will be okay. It fuels my courage to keep going. I know that I am connected to Him and He is carrying me safely through the unknowns of it all.

Just as I became familiar with and learned to lean into each phase of the migraine, I have learned to lean into the different stages of the grieving process and God's healing process.

And one thing is for sure: There is no way to go around it. You've got to go *through* it.

* * *

Reflections

"There is no greater agony than bearing an untold story inside of you." – Maya Angelou

As you reflect on the chapter, consider the challenges you face in your own life. Is there a recurring difficulty that you find yourself grappling with? Reflect on how you navigate through these moments and the ways you find gratitude when you emerge on the other side.

This is a space provided for you to explore these questions further. Allow your thoughts and feelings to flow freely.

Tell your story – it matters.

If you need more room to write, I invite you to continue in your journal

Chapter 2

Seasons of Change

*"The seasons change and you change,
but the Lord abides evermore the same,
and the streams of His love are deep,
as broad and as full as ever."*

– Charles Spurgeon

I was born and raised on a farm in the rural quiet countryside of Berkley, (near Huntsville) Alabama with my mother, father, sister and brothers. At age 12, I was living in the city of Long Beach, California with my mother, sister and brothers.

I was around 18 years old when I met my future husband, McArthur Lavender. It was the summer after I graduated high school. I was living at home with my mother, who managed the apartment building. Mac and his cousin were tenants in the building. Mac was born and raised in the rural countryside of Eutaw, (near Tuscaloosa) Alabama. I was infatuated with this handsome man at first sight. We would say hello and make small talk, until one day, he asked me out on a date. Our first date was going to an outside drive-in movie theater. I think the movie was "Shaft". We dated for a while, then he went back to Chicago. But from there, he would write me love letters. One day, he returned and asked me to be his wife. I still have those letters over 50 years later and read them from time to time.

I lovingly called him Mac. He acquired the nickname "Peewee" as a child, and it gained momentum as a popular and skilled basketball player. The nickname stuck with him for a lifetime.

* * *

I was 22 on our wedding day. My brother, Robert (RIP), escorted me down the aisle. We stood in front of Rev. Ford. Standing with us were my maid of honor (my sister Stephanie), and bridesmaids (my sister Dorothy, my niece, Faye, and my cousins Jean and Sharon), Best man Kenny (RIP), the groomsmen (Mitch, Brothers Emanuel and Sylvester, Cousin James (RIP)), Ring bearer (nephew Russell), Flower girl Lena (RIP) and my bonus son, Troy. We recited the traditional vows, looking into each other's eyes, "For better or worse, in sickness and health, till death do us part!" And the responses we gave to Pastor Ford: I do. I do. And our journey began as husband and wife.

A few years passed. We had three children. Life, work, play, church, with their good, bad and ugly scenes. Suddenly, we were empty nesters, and had a baker's dozen of grandchildren.

We grew older, trying to keep going at the same pace of life as we did when we were younger. Operating on auto-pilot mode, every day pretty much the same, rising early, off to work, coming home late; and the weekends just as routine as the weekdays. I knew it was time for a change. Mac is 63 and I'm 51, married for 30 years. We start to seriously look to the future, what's next? Being a visionary, I was always looking to the future, it was hard to live in the moment. I ask myself, Is this it? Just more of the same.

* * *

In the spring of 2006, I was visiting my family in Omaha. On a whim, my sister and I decided to go to open houses and I fell in love with a home and property. It was my spacious dream home that backed up to the woods. Beyond the woods was the beautiful Lake Cunningham. I convinced Mac that this would be the perfect vacation home. That we should try on the midwest and see what that would look like, feel like, smell like, taste like. Perhaps this could be our retirement home. Seeing the photos and my enthusiasm, he was on board to submit an offer without having ever set foot on the property. We purchase our home!

Although we both were from Alabama, living a few hundred miles apart, we met, got married and lived in southern California ever since. The sunny weather, the California lifestyle, the beach nearby – it attracted a lot of people to migrate to the state. But we rarely took advantage of our location. We were starting to feel stuck within the circle of familiarity. Now that we had the option, the question for us was: could we voluntarily leave it all?

Our biggest concern was not being close to our sons, daughter and grandchildren. This was where we had always lived, where our children were born and raised, where our friends were, our stable community, traditional church where I had been since I was 12 years old. We had built and known this lifestyle from day 1 of our marriage. It was really comfortable and safe here, just like the career I had been in for the past 30 years.

Yet I had a strong desire for us to break away, spend time together without all of the familiar. In the back of my mind, I was tired of what I call the congested concrete haven – the hustle and bustle California freeway lifestyles. There were so many freeway options 5, 10, 15, 22, 105, 110, 210, 215, 405, 605 and more! I simply longed for a simple interstate lifestyle of the 80 and 680; or even a two-lane highway, or country dirt road lifestyle.

Time and life were moving so fast, and we really wanted a slower pace of life. We weighed the pros and cons. One of the great benefits was knowing Mac would be within a 6-hour drive to his brothers in Chicago and they would have an opportunity to visit more often. It brings me great joy and heart smiles knowing they spent so much quality time with each other because of this decision.

* * *

It was 4 years after purchasing the home, that we both retired, on the same day and found ourselves home together, 24/7. That was a challenge for both of us, since this was the most time we had ever spent together and it took quite a bit of adjusting.

We worked out the hiccups and adjusted into retirement life. It became our new normal, which I now see was a precursor, a foretelling to the many new normals that would lie ahead.

We immediately put into motion our plan to move into our Omaha home with the attitude of 'let it last as long as it lasts'.

Fast forward to June 2010, we packed boxes and loaded the 20-foot U-Haul. Mac, Chris, and our grandson Chris Jr. drove the truck and car across the country to begin our new season of life. A place to embrace changing seasons of the year, as well as life, literally and figuratively. We had new scenery and the changing seasons, which demarcated the passing of time – summer turning into fall, fall into winter, and winter to spring. I recognized that we were entering the 'fall' season of our lives.

I wondered about what was next and was excited and ready for it.

* * *

We settled into a quiet lifestyle, gardening and spending time together. He spent a lot of time working in the yard, mowing on his new John Deere riding mower, watching classic western TV shows, playing solitaire, sitting in the garage, and waving as people in cars passed by. He spent time with his new friends on Friday evenings.

After a while, we found a new familiar. We had a new community. I found the perfect church and loved Omaha. We took every opportunity to visit more often with our Chicago, St. Louis, and Alabama family. We still visited often with our California family. In the summers, the grandchildren would visit us. We intentionally created beautiful memories for them in a place full of nature – going to the lake, enjoying the open spaces, and taking full advantage of our new found freedom in the suburbs of Lake Cunnigham. In the winters, we became snowbirds and spent most of our time in sunny California. We were very blessed to have the best of both worlds for over 10 years.

Looking back, we had happily left California without reservations, knowing that Omaha was not our forever home and we had the option to return whenever we chose. We left our California home vacant for a while, rented it out for a while, then converted it to an Airbnb. This arrangement was working perfectly. Little did I know, 10 years later, like clockwork, it would not be our timing – but our *destiny* – to return to California. It was not under the conditions that we had envisioned or planned. It was all in God's master plan.

* * *

In the winter of 2019, we were approaching our tenth year in Omaha. We had decided not to be snowbirds this season. Rather than escaping to California, we were resolved to enjoy the winter months, equipped with all the snow tools, equipment and gear that we needed to hibernate for the brutal Omaha winter. Two of the grandkids, Chris Jr. and Amajay came to spend the Christmas break with us. There was lots of snow, which they enjoyed thoroughly and, of course, we did too.

On New Year's Eve, it was tradition to celebrate at my sister and brother-in-law's house. They would have an old-school party with family and friends. The house would be decorated with black, gold, and silver. Even the plates, cups, hats and whistles, and horns would match the theme. We got all dolled up!

It was always a fun evening, Stephanie would cook a spread of food – chicken, spaghetti and a variety of dips. Paul would DJ and ensure there were a variety of drinks. Laughter, old school music, dancing in the basement, and of course, taking lots of photos. Adults and kids. Family and friends.

This year was extra special. We had our two grandsons with us. Mac was the life of the party, telling his jokes, the same jokes he had told year after year, as long as I have known him. Not only would the people listening laugh, but he would laugh heartily at his own jokes. This year was one of the best!

There was a photo booth set aside. Mac and I went in to take pictures together. Just as we were finishing a photo, he took a moment, made a toast and said "Happy New Year Mrs. Lavender", kissed me, and said "who loves you baby".

At midnight, we blew horns, toasted aloud "Happy New Year", hugged each other and we could hear the guns firing outside. We bundled up and left about 2 am, after all the cacophony had calmed down. We felt the brutal cold the second we stepped out of the house. There was snow and ice on the windshields. We said good night and headed home.

Jr. and Amajay, went back to California a few days later.

* * *

Fast forward to 2020. We were making a lot of assumptions and presumptions, taking it for granted that this would be the best year ever – 2020! It was going to be a year of 20/20 vision. I had already created my vision board and my goals were visible, plain and clear for all to see.

In early January, there were rumblings of a plague. A pandemic. What's that? It can't be serious. None of the leaders had acknowledged it, and life was going on as normal, so I figured there must not be much to it. In January, the rumors started to get louder. A few cases were reported here and there of a virus called Covid-19, and there were deaths tied to it. It was like a pink polka-dotted elephant in the room and no one really wanted to talk about it. Yet, it controlled our actions and we could feel a reserved panic.

But, I did what I normally do – I ignored it. Surely if I ignore it, it will simply go away, right? It may affect other folks, but not me, or us. Not the secured United States. Not my community. Not my home.

As I heard the news reports of how serious it actually was, little did I know it was the beginning of life-changing seasons and events for everyone with a ripple effect that lingers on, even years later.

* * *

In February, our daughter asked us to come to California and babysit, because her birthday was coming soon. We said yes, packing lightly since we planned to return home in 2 weeks.

We each took one small piece of luggage. This was the lightest I had ever traveled!

On our previous snowbird trips, I would tug several 50-pound bags onto Southwest Airlines. Since we could take two bags each for free, I took complete advantage and packed 200 lbs of stuff and things between the two of us. I always included my books. Everything but the kitchen sink!

Mac would always complain, "why do you need all this stuff?"

"Because we are staying for months and I may need it all!"

He would weigh each luggage and ensure it was under 50 pounds and we would lug it to the airport. After all, we were snowbirds, and I needed my library.

This time, however, we were ready to travel light for a quick two-week trip. I had canceled the scheduled guest who had reservations at our Airbnb and blocked the time for us through March 10. It was Feb 18, that we boarded the flight from Omaha, connecting in Denver on to Long Beach, California.

We arrived in California, with more and more talk about Covid. This virus thing on every news channel, in every conversation. It had everyone's full attention. People were starting to die all over the world. It was a global pandemic! There was uncertainty, panic and a whole lot of concern about what we, as humans, were up against.

It became official on March 16. Everyone around the world was told to stay home in lockdown, and everything but the grocery stores had shut down.

* * *

Mac and I decided to stay in Long Beach, to hunker down at the Airbnb until this was over. We were happy to be near our family, we had nothing to rush back to in Omaha and it was the best place to be. A couple of months after the lockdown, we were all stocked up in preparation. We stayed inside with no visitors, except when our sons, Chris or Jason stopped by to bring things to refill our pantry. We felt we were in a pretty secure place.

But all of this was the calm before the storm.

Reflections

Looking back at the ups and downs of life, I see Romans 8:28 at work in its finest details; "And we know that all things work together for good to those who love God, to those who are called according to His purpose."

What's your life story in a snapshot? Using as much or as little detail as you like, capture your story. Major life events, special moments, and milestones.

What was your normal life like before the loss of your loved one? Visualize what your life was like when your loved one was in it and write down the snapshot of your life when you felt it was normal.

What stands out in your memory of what normal felt like and looked like?

Tell your story – it matters.

If you need more room to write, I invite you to continue in your journal

Chapter 3

In The Blink Of An Eye

*"We do not remember days,
we remember moments."*
—Cesare Pavese

On Saturday evening – 23rd May, 2020 to be exact – Mac and I were downstairs, after dinner, watching a movie "The Upside" with Kevin Hart. Mac was sitting at the table and I was lying down on the sofa.

Out of the blue, he said "You know what, we are on our last leg, and we have no one to take care of us, it's just me and you."

I was not in the mood to entertain that kind of conversation, especially after a Kevin Hart movie. So I made a smart alec retort and said, "You may not have anyone, but I do. We have our children, we are near family. And we do have each other."

And with that, it was the end of that discussion and we moved on to other topics.

I regret that. I wish I had dug deeper and found out what was on his mind. What was the point that he was making with that statement "We are on our last leg"?

This conversation was prophetic because of what was soon to unfold.

***

The next morning was the fourth Sunday of May 2020. At about 8:30 in the morning, things had started to stir around our house. It was just the two of us. 6-7 weeks into the lockdown. We had adjusted to the new norm of living in a pandemic, sleeping in the second bedroom of our California home. We had left the primary bedroom for Airbnb guests.

Mac and I had been awake for a while, doing the normal morning routines. He had just walked back and sat on the side of the bed, then he casually laid in bed. I asked him a couple of questions about breakfast. Are you hungry? Do you want a cup of tea? Why don't you go downstairs and make the tea this morning?

We had a spat for a minute, rather, I should say, I was doing most of the petty talking in anticipation of what I knew were his typical responses. I knew that it was early in the day and he didn't normally have a lot to say until the afternoon.

He was giving me one-word answers. I was hoping he would go downstairs this morning. I was delaying the inevitable – I would have to go make breakfast and bring it back up. I said, "Well, you go and make the tea this morning and I will make breakfast later".

"No, you do it. I don't feel like it."

"Well, I guess we won't be having tea this morning!"

I was playing hardball to see if he would volunteer to go downstairs. He had moved from sitting on the side of the bed, laying back on his single pillow. This was normal. I did the same – I laid back and turned to Facebook, scrolling, lining up the church services that we attended remotely each Sunday on my phone.

It was the same routine we had every Sunday since the pandemic – to attend church services online, just as we were, in our pajamas, in bed, on the phone. Viewing Pastor Shaw at 8:30 am, then Pastor Kim at 9:30 am, and Pastor Sean at 11 am. We looked forward to hearing the sermon. I watched as Pastor Shaw stood in front of the podium, praying. Then he began speaking, preaching the word. Listening to church online was one of the new normals that connected us back to the familiarity of church and God's word.

I sat up in bed with two pillows behind my back, my head

looking down, pen in hand. I was taking copious notes to capture the parts of the message that were intended for me.

I noticed out of the corner of my eye that Mac was lying back on his pillow, listening, quietly taking it all in. It made my heart happy to see him doing this. Nothing unusual about this.

It came to a point in the sermon when Pastor Shaw said *"Keep on living, going to get old, going to get feeble and going to need strength, going to go through this in marriage, with children and you are going to need God. His strength; He is our very present help in times of trouble..."*

It was then that Mac responded in a low tone, "That's right". This was unusual and out of character for him; normally he doesn't say a word. He just listens. I finished taking the note and turned my head to the left towards the wall nearest me and then to the right towards Mac.

He lay there, motionless – eyes open, arms slightly raised and bent, fists clenched.

He was catatonic and unresponsive.

I began yelling and screaming his name. I jumped up, screaming and ran over to his side of the bed, near the window. I shook him, but he didn't budge or say a word.

"Peewee, Peewee!" I yelled and screamed and ran downstairs,

in my pj's or whatever I had on, I'm not sure to this day. I ran to my next-door neighbor, banging on the door with both hands. He answered, and all I could do was say help me. Help me!

"Do you want me to call 911?"

Yes. Yes, yes.

I went to my other next-door neighbor who I knew well, and *bam bam bam* on the door. No one answered at first. As I was running back to my house, he came out.

I was out of breath. All I could do was beckon, for him to follow me.

I ran up the stairs, with both my neighbors following me.

Sean stood with me in the bedroom and Joe stood on the landing talking with 911. Then he handed me his phone.

The woman on the line asked me if he was still breathing, and if he was warm. I touched him and said yes, he is warm, but I don't think he is breathing.

She calmly and urgently said, "Someone is on the way; you will need to give him CPR."

She walked me through what to do – push on his chest and breathe into his mouth, over and over. My mouth covered his, blowing my breath into his mouth, watching his non-responsive body.

I did the best I could do, as the lady said; "over and over again",

At one point, I asked her "Where are you? What is taking them so long?"

The other neighbors had gathered outside. One of them took my phone and called my son and daughter.

The paramedics, the fire department, and the sheriffs arrived all at once and rushed into the room. They sent me and the neighbors out of the room as they started working on my husband. My daughter arrived and went upstairs. I followed her, and we made it to the landing, where the lady sheriff officer was posted.

She said, "You do not want to go into the room. You do not want to see what they are doing. You do not want to have that image in your head, in every room you enter, for the rest of your life."

I believed her.

So we back outside the house, left with no choice but to wait. I melted into my daughter's arms, sobbing as she consoled me. Jason, my oldest son, and his wife soon arrived. We were all in shock. It was as though everything was in slow-motion.

We continued to wait outside for about 40 minutes, while they worked on my husband.

Finally, they brought him down the stairs on a stretcher.

My mind is very foggy about certain details of that day, while others I remember clearly. It was a blur but snapshots are still clear as day. I do not recall what he looked like, but I know he didn't have a shirt on and there were round sticker tapes on his chest. He also had an oxygen mask on him. Why would he need that? Surely he must have been breathing.

As they were putting him into the ambulance, I asked to ride with him, but they refused. They took him to the local hospital, only a few blocks away. I distinctly recall there was no siren at any point.

* * *

I slipped into autopilot mode, trying to be strong for everyone around me. My daughter drove me to the hospital and I called Pastor Kim along the way and explained the situation. "I'll be right there", she said. She was at the hospital within minutes of our arrival.

For me, it is clear that Peewee had passed away on that day, May 24, 2020. Although officially he passed away and was pronounced dead on Jun 7, 2020 at 9:05 pm.

It was in the blink of an eye that he was gone.

He never recovered from the massive heart attack he had had that morning.

Reflections

Looking back, I regret not listening and digging deeper and finding out what was on his mind the night before his heart attack. What was the point that he was making with that statement "We are on our last leg"? Things really change in the blink of an eye, all of a sudden life is changed forever.

When did you first hear of your loved ones passing? What is your story? How did you feel, what did you do, where were you, when did it happen, what stands out in your mind about that day?

Do you feel that you have allowed yourself to go through grieving for your loved one?

Do you have true regrets that were not resolved before your loved one passed?

Tell your story – it matters.

If you need more room to write, I invite you to continue in your journal

Chapter 4

The Toughest Decision Of My Life

"Remember, letting go isn't about having the courage to release the past; It is about having the wisdom and strength to embrace the present."
– Marc & Angel

We hurried to the emergency room, with masks on, the security posted at the door, cleared to go up to the window. My heart was racing, I said "Lavender was just brought into emergency, and we want to go back and see what is going on with him". As they asked a few questions, talking among themselves, I clearly heard one of them say, "He's the code blue".

I was operating on adrenaline, I said I wanted to go back and see him. After some more background talk, and a few minutes passed, they unlocked the door and Ginger and I were allowed to enter. Peewee was in the room, his eyes were closed with an oxygen machine pumping, and he seemed to respond when

Ginger called out Dad, Dad, and I said Peewee. I don't recall a lot of this time, it's a big blur.

Soon afterwards, we were asked to leave the room and go out to the waiting room, which was set up outside the building, with some chairs. It was at the height of the pandemic and no one was allowed to go beyond this point. I looked out further away and standing in the parking lot were Pastor Kim and Minister Janice. After a while, the doctor called for me, and gave an update on my husband's status and prognosis.

As my daughter and I listened, I understood that he was in critical condition. I gave permission and signed papers to get him the treatments he needed to survive. He was placed into a medically induced coma with his body temperature lowered to 33 degrees, where he would remain for a period of 48 hours. The doctor's plan, and our prayer, was that when they warmed him back up, he would recover without brain damage. He remained in the ICU and we prayed and asked others to pray with us.

The doctor told me "The nurses may try to stop you, but if you need *anything*, just call me. He gave us his phone number. I did take him up on the offer once, but it was not necessary at any point afterward during his stay for the next two weeks. We had unlimited access to visits. This was a blessing, a gift from God that I am grateful for.

There were heavy restrictions at all the hospitals during the pandemic, so they were only allowing two of us to pair up and go in the room at a time.

Ginger, Jason and Chris (my children) and I paired up to see him. Then we switched up and then we would go one by one. He was lying there on a ventilator machine, unconscious, as the team of doctors and nurses came to monitor him. They offered updates and we asked questions. Each one of us talked openly with Mac, as though he was conscious, letting him know we loved him.

"I love you"

"It's going to be okay"

"Do you hear me?"

I would pull up the chair near the bed and sit, holding his hand, waiting and expecting that any second, he would regain consciousness, wake up, and come back to us.

I didn't know it then, but have since found studies that indicate there is evidence that talking to your loved one while in a coma is comforting to them and can help with recovery. According to Traditional Health "During a coma, the individual is unconscious, meaning they are unable to respond to any sounds. However, the brain may still be able to pick up on sounds from loved ones. In fact, some studies suggest talking and touching a loved one while they are in a coma may help them recover."

This is exactly what we were doing instinctively. And I believe that he heard us.

In shock and disbelief in all that had happened on this Sunday, we stayed near him and each other throughout the night.

When I returned home that night, I saw that the first responders had left behind on Mac's night stand, a heart monitor reading tape. It showed sporadic heart beats and even a flat line. The tape read ID Patient 7083; Patient Mode: Adult: 5/24/2020 09.19.3

* * *

On Tuesday, May 26, 2020, 48 hours after the induced coma, the doctors decided it was time to bring him back. We had asked everyone to pray at 2 PM, when his temperature would be returned to normal and he would be taken off the sedatives. They started the process and we kept track of time. We stood by his side, hour by hour, hoping and praying to see him open his eyes, to respond to us, or to even move.

48 hours had passed, and unfortunately, the response the doctors sought and we prayed for were not evident.

In the days that followed, the doctors gave their diagnosis.

He was brain-dead. Essentially, he could live as a vegetable in a convalescent home with the functions of a 6-month old, with feeding tubes. Or we could decide to take him off of life support.

The doctor informed us that we needed to make a decision by Friday – two days from that point. But I felt, wanted, needed more time and asked them to wait until Sunday. The doctors agreed. I knew that if there were no improvements, then I would face the hardest decision of my life.

We asked the family to 'meet' him through a Zoom meeting. Family from Omaha, Chicago, Atlanta, and Long Beach joined us remotely. They could see him, in the hospital bed, and on a ventilator. I wanted to let him hear their voices. As I watched his face for any sign that he was listening, I could hear what they were saying to him

"Hey Peewee"
"We are praying for you, Mac",
"We are waiting for you"
"We need you back here, man"

During the call, the doctor came into the room. Before he gave the update, I asked Pastor Kim to pray. We ended the call.

The doctor reaffirmed the critical condition.

It was a tiring day. I was exhausted.

I was *going through*.

I went home. I walked upstairs and laid across our bed. I tried to get some rest, but sleep was eluding me. My mind and heart was racing from one thing to the next. I closed my eyes, and in between cat naps, I prayed that he would be healed and come back home. I truly could not imagine that he would not be coming back home and that I would have to go on living my life without him.

* * *

Looking back: Continuously I prayed, had conversations with the LORD God "Lord, touch and heal my husband, please allow him to come home"; "Lord have mercy"; "Help me Lord"; "Lead me Lord, "; "Father, I need you Lord"; "Show me the way Father", "What am I to do, Lord?" And He led me with peace during some of the hardest moments of my life.

* * *

The next day was a rollercoaster.

I went back to the hospital and up to Mac's room. When I talked to him, I saw a flutter of his eye lids and wanted to think I saw some mouth movement. I believed he was trying to come back. However, the doctors told me he remained the same with no change – in a comatose state, in critical condition, with a host of medical issues. His reactions were not what the doctors needed to see. They indicated brain damage.

As Sunday approached, we remained anchored with hope and we believed in miracles.

On Saturday, I updated my family and friends that Mac was still in a comatose state. We continued to pray for his healing for full recovery and that he would come home with me.

* * *

It was exactly 7 days since his massive heart attack, around the same hour. I woke up that morning feeling good. I felt calm, infused with perfect peace. It was as though there had been a surge of strength and courage.

As I was lying across my bed, looking at his clothes, his watch and his cap on the nightstand, I had a knowing that surpassed the realities of the day. I knew so many people were praying. I knew God answered prayers and His will would prevail.

As Mac's condition remained unchanged and I faced the toughest decision of my life, I trusted my faith and followed my peace in the midst of all that was going on.

I knew what Mac would want. We had talked about this many times before. We had our final wishes formalized in a trust. He would not want to live the life that was described to us. Not only would Peewee have said no to living in a vegetative state on a ventilator, he would have said "Hell no!", with more explicit language to follow.

Looking back, I see that all of this gave me solace and in my heart of hearts, I was assured that God was in control. He had already taken him home. Further details and explanations are neither required nor necessary. *Release him and let him go home*, was the order I received in my spirit.

I was willing to comply with his wishes. It is my hope that when my time comes, my loved ones will comply with mine.

* * *

In the message that Pastor Shaw was preaching – when Mac said his last words, "That's right" – he said keep on living. You're going to get old, going to get feverish and going to need strength. You're going to go through things in marriage and with children and you're going to need God.

How prophetic that message was and the scripture was for Mac and even more so for me at this moment, in the decisions that must be made.

All I can say is "I know that's right".

PSALM 46:1
God is our refuge and strength, A very present help in trouble.

PSALM 46:10
Be still, and know that I am God

* * *

The beach, the ocean, is one of the most peaceful places that I know. It has been and remains one of my favorite places to go to be in the moment, to meditate and find joy.

I called for a family meeting. I asked Ginger, Chris and Jason to meet me at the beach. Around noon that day, Ginger/Keron, Jason/Nicole, Chris/Paula and I met at Cherry beach. We tracked through the sand, dipped our feet in the cool ocean water, smiling and praying.

The ocean waves rolled in and out, mirroring our emotional waves. We had light moments, we laughed together, we joined hands and prayed together, we cried together as we talked about their dad and his condition. We reminisced, we hugged, and even argued about whether it was time to let him go.

Every emotion flooded through our family – some wanted to honor his wishes, while others felt the need to hold on to him. Some just kept silent. I knew what he wanted, I had perfect peace in the middle of this storm. I voiced our decision.

With sandy feet and a new perspective, we went back to the hospital and went upstairs to inform the doctors of our decision. It was on me. I was Mac's spokesperson. We were sad. We stood in a circle, holding hands. While we were not ready to let go, God knew every heart. He allowed us to be on one accord and move forward together.

*　*　*

It was time.

Only two of us could go into the room and visit with Mac at a time. I went up to his room first. I stood by his bed, held his hand, brushed his brow, kissed his cheek and said "I know you left me the other Sunday. This machine has been doing your breathing for you ever since. I know your wishes. God has spoken, and I know."

After a while, one by one, Ginger, then Chris and then Jason came up to spend time with their dad.

I looked at the monitor of the ventilator. We had been told that if the reading is over 21, Mac is breathing partially on his own. If it was 20 or under, the machine was mostly breathing for him.

The number was under 20.

Critical decisions must be made today. A pulmonary doctor and neurologist both confirmed his declining condition and dire prognosis. I was at peace with our decision so I informed the doctor.

At 1:48 pm, the nurse on duty came in to remove his breathing tubes. I witnessed her doing so and then she finally turned off the machine. Thus he officially began the end of his human journey. It was surreal and so very real. A supernatural and perfectly natural experience, all at once.

* * *

On Tuesday, June 2nd, 2020, Mac had been off the ventilator for a few days. My son and I were sitting with him, talking to him, when suddenly, his eyes seemed to open.

I didn't know what that meant. I was hoping and praying this was a sign of recovery, an answer to prayers, the miracle that so many of us were still praying for. We witnessed several more body reactions throughout the day that we were viewing as improvements – this was a glimpse of hope for us all!

We asked to talk to the doctors. The next day, we met with 3 of his doctors and we received their reports that he was not doing well at all. There had been no progress or activity. He had no cognitive function and all the doctors gave medical explanations for his movements. Then they affirmed and detailed his irreversible state.

* * *

People would ask me "How are you doing?" and I would say "I'm okay" – whatever that meant. I was kind of numb and it felt surreal. But I knew Mac, and it was going to be okay.

Mac's 78th birthday fell on Friday, June 5th 2020. I brought birthday decorations for Peewee's room. I tied the tag on his tube and wrote Peewee's name on a birthday cap, placing it on his bed. I wanted the nurses, doctors, whoever came into the ICU room to know it was his birthday. I wanted them to say Happy Birthday to Mr. Lavender.

It all felt so strange. While in the room, I still hoped and prayed for a miracle.

I posted happy birthday to him on social media. Our friends and family helped me wish him. Most of them had no idea that he was lying in an ICU bed at the hospital.

* * *

At the height of the pandemic, families were not allowed to visit loved ones at the hospital. But we were given unlimited permission to visit Peewee, to be at his side, to hold his hand, to whisper in his ear, and talk with him. To say our goodbyes. The doctor gave us his phone number and assured me that even though the nurses may try to stop us, we could contact him directly and he would give us permission. I had to make this call to the doctor once, but it was not necessary at any point after that.

This was a blessing, a gift from God that I am grateful for. God allowed us two solid weeks to say goodbye to Mac. He blessed us with this favor during the pandemic. He gave us peace beyond understanding.

* * *

It was 9:05 pm on Sunday, June 7, I was home in bed and Chris was downstairs. The phone rang. I picked it up and saw the caller ID: *Lakewood Hospital.*

I knew right away that it was the dreaded phone call. I answered and the woman on the other end proceeded to say "Is this Gwen Lavender?"

I responded "Yes."

"We are sorry to inform you – your husband has just passed".

My heart sank, I told her we would be right there, and yelled for Chris.

Chris drove me over to the hospital, entering through the emergency entrance, where security would only allow one person at a time to go up and see him. I chose to go first. I walked through the door, down the long hall to the elevator, took the elevator to the 3rd floor. I walked down to where the nurse met me in the hall. She escorted me into this quiet room. There were sterile white curtains and white sheets. Mac was lying there.

Reality hit home and my heart broke when I saw him. It was almost unbearable. "I was going through". Moments later, I looked up and Chris was walking in the room. He came over and wrapped his arms around me. God knew I needed some help through this moment. The nurse had called security to take permission that allowed him to come up. Both of us could be in the room with Mac at the same time.

We spent our final moments with him. The details of what happened after are a blur. Then we left him at the hospital.

Later that evening, the entire family gathered and we all stayed under one roof for the next few weeks.

Reflections

As I look back, this was one of the weakest days on my grief journey. It broke my heart to hear Peewee's prognosis from the doctors. It breaks my heart today as I share with you. It hurts. There is nothing easy about it. It's difficult and painful.
Now I know, unaware at the time that I was strengthened then and now, as I rely on my faith and God's Word that was in my heart. I was clinging to 2 Corinthians 12:9 "And He said to me, "My grace is sufficient for you, for My strength is made perfect in weakness."

Have you ever been faced with making a tough decision? How did you handle it?

When you look back now, what helped you and sustained you in making that decision?

What were some moments that were gifted to you during this time?

Tell your story – it matters.

If you need more room to write, I invite you to continue in your journal

Chapter 5

A Farewell With Love

"To live in hearts we leave behind is not to die."
— Thomas Campbell

As we struggled with Peewee's passing, everyone in the family mourned. We suffered and each expressed grief in our own unique ways. The children grieved. The grandchildren grieved. It affected each of us in different ways and only they can tell their unique story, as only I can tell mine and you can tell yours.

During the two-week period after Mac's passing, Ginger took the lead in handling all the business and coordinating affairs. She also took care of me by ensuring that all of my wishes were heard and made sure that I had opportunities to rest, even though, all the while, she was silently grieving the loss of her dad.

Chris made sure his friends were pallbearers and handled intricate details that he knew his pops would appreciate, even as he pressed through the stronghold of grief and contended with the disbelief that pops was gone.

Jason acted as the priest of the family. He vocally prayed and interceded for his dad. He kept the family grounded in prayer, anchored in hope and faith that his dad would be healed and fully recover, despite the circumstances that tore at the depths of his heart.

From across the country, Troy stayed in touch throughout each day, providing the level-headed support in the decision-making through it all, as he grieved the loss of his father.

I shall never forget how Pastor Kim and Minister Janice supported our family, even though I was not a full time member of the church. Each request that I made of Pastor Kim, her response was "no problem". She brought the eulogy and Minister Janice sang at the graveside service.

Even in the midst of the pandemic, our family and friends supported me in every way they could – a true village. I didn't even have to ask and they never missed a beat. Like the petals of a rose opening, everything just naturally unfolded.

My dear friend, Dr. Sandra Hardy would touch base with me throughout the day, morning, noon and night. When I would walk to the hospital, she would meet me halfway and we would walk in silence at times, and other times, talk and pray. Her being there, her presence, was like the air I breathed. Oftentimes she would just text me:

"Calling to let you know, you are thought of today"
"How's your day? Remember to BREATHE. It's okay."
"How can I be a good friend to you today?"

This was simple and seamless. She was my confidante. Oftentimes, I didn't know what I needed, but she was there with me in my silence. She was right there ready to listen and came along beside me to sit in stillness. She was an angel friend that God placed in my life to help me through this difficult time, to walk by my side.

Right away my brother, Emanuel hopped into his car and drove 1400 miles from Omaha to be by my side. My sister, Stephanie and niece, Jamila flew in from Omaha. My brother-in-law, Nell, came in from Chicago. My nephew, Derrick from Vegas. All of them showed up in the middle of the pandemic. My family was surrounded by the love of God. A strong presence of community was ever-present. At a time when the world had come to a halt due to the pandemic, when there was a long waiting list to be scheduled with mortuaries, when the only option was to have a graveside service, with months of waiting to even have a service – we experienced none of that. We were able to have a viewing at the chapel with some guidelines to wear a mask and maintain distance. I believe Mac would have been pleased with all that happened that day.

Our dear friends Jackie and Sharon, they were key in making things happen behind the scenes. At the graveside service, I looked up and there they were standing in the distant background and as the weeks followed they were there supporting and surrounding me with love.

* * *

I am of African royalty, and I heard the calling of an unknown tradition for this part of the service. It was very important to me to follow my heart, my vision. As we began to plan Mac's service, I knew I wanted to wear a grand African headdress.

However, I didn't have a headdress. My friend Lilypat in Omaha was a seamstress and fashion model. I texted her a few days after Mac passed and told her my vision. She told me she was in Africa, but she called her daughter and her daughter called my sister. They met up in Omaha and she ensured my sister had the headdress to bring with her when she came for the services. I was honored that Lilypat went through all the effort to make my vision come true. The headdress was beautiful!

On June 18, 2020, we held the viewing service at the chapel followed by a graveside service. We all huddled in a big family car and arrived at the chapel for the viewing before everyone else. Our family wore white and I wore my purple African headdress.

We had printed out the obituary for every guest, which included a snapshot of his life, family pictures, and tributes from some of the family members.

In it, I wrote this note to the love of my life:

Dear Peewee,

I miss you so much.
We have loved each other for nearly 50 years.
I don't know how I'm going to do it without you.
Although you never told me directly, I now realize you were tired and you went home.
I will see you in the morning sweetheart.
Love and cherish, we vowed, to death do us part, and we did it.
As I think back, we were unlikely matches; opposites. But you caught my eye and I caught yours and God said yes!
We did it.
You covered me and I covered you and God covered us both And we loved each other.

As the chapel service began, Pastor Kim made opening remarks and emphasized social distancing. She then began the prayer. At first, I sat in the front row with our sons and daughter. After a while, I stood at the head of the casket, accepting condolences and comforting my family, asking how they were doing. I felt empowered by God, wearing my beautiful headdress, like a queen and my husband as my king. I felt calm and at peace.

There was silence in the room. As people entered, some immediately took a seat, while others walked up to the casket for the viewing and gave a nod of acknowledgement before sitting down. Sporadically, family and friends began to get up, go to the front of the chapel, up to the podium to speak of memories with Mac.

Bob, Mac's former boss, talked about the years he and Mac had worked together. A long time friend talked of the years they played softball together at King's park. Another talked about how he was a great basketball player. Yet another friend complimented Mac's singing in the Men's choir.

Our granddaughter, Staesha, spoke of how her grandpa would dare the grandkids to do a certain thing again, and that was his way of saying that's enough, don't do it again. The way she told the story led to a chuckle from the audience. Almost all the memories shared invoked smiles, chuckles and some laughter. That's the kind of person Mac was.

I said a few words and thanked everyone for coming.

When it was time to leave for the cemetery the mortician whispered in my ear, "Would you like to close the casket?" and without hesitation, I said yes.
I looked at Mac's face, knowing that I would never see him again on this side of heaven.

"I will see you in the morning, my love." ...and slowly closed the lid.

That was it. This was our final goodbye.

* * *

After leaving the chapel, we caravanned to the cemetery. I remember looking around and seeing my entire family together; the oldest to the youngest grandkids (Jaylen, Staesha, Jr, Tyler, Jeff, Amajay, Kameron, Abby and Cailee) dressed in white and friends from different seasons of our life. My brother, Sylvester started the service with prayer. Then family friend, Nikki, read the obituary, Minister Janice sang a song and the eulogy and benediction was done by Pastor Kim. The service ended with a beautiful white dove release. We stood in a semi-circle holding the fluttering doves, waiting until all the grandchildren had theirs in hand. I said a few words, looked up to the sky and let go of the first doves and the others let go of theirs. We watched until they flew in a formation, out of our sight.

The program and the beautiful white doves so perfectly reflected my wishes.

I looked around, there were so many people at the service. As much as people made the effort to social distance, there were still hugs and handshakes. We stayed through the burial and lingered around. The services were beautiful and to this day, it serves as one of my most special memories.

We sat at the gravesite for a while until someone said, "I think we should leave."

We caravanned back to my house for the repass. My neighbors Carla and Myoshi catered the food and everything was all set when we arrived.

* * *

Looking back now, I realize I did not openly weep. As I think about it, I would describe myself as stoic. Empowered with supernatural strength, I was standing at the head of the casket accepting condolences and comforting my family, asking how they were doing. I acted and felt like I was operating outside of myself, empowered. It was unreal to me. The Lord carried me through the day, full of grace and strength.

In the weeks that followed, Lord, my life was so different. My world had turned upside down and I was in a strange place, living in unfamiliar surroundings.

Starting a new journey without my husband was a lonely time. He had been my companion for more than 45 years. He was my soul mate. My better half. He was gone and I thought I didn't know where he was.

Now that I didn't have him anymore, I felt as though half my body was missing. I felt as though the right side of my body was gone and I walked around with a limp. A wobble. Like half a person. For a while, I even felt the need to walk with a cane to maintain my balance.

I had grown so accustomed to having him by my side, calling my name for this and that – Mrs. Lavender, Gwen, sweetheart, who loves you, baby. He was a good man, and I wish I could have him back, flaws and all. Now, there's no one to check on me, love me the way he did, or rub my feet. When I have migraine attacks, there's no one to ask how I'm doing. I look over to his side of the bed, and it's empty.

Oh, the things I took for granted!

I felt the same way after the loss of my mother. I remember feeling like I had no one left to pray for me. Then, God sent one of my mother's dear friends, Mrs. Wade, into my life. She told me something I will never forget. Before my mother passed, she had asked her friend to pray for me and all her children. She had our names on her prayer list and she prayed for us each day.

God also showed me that I needed to learn to pray for myself and for others, and that there were people praying for me, even when I didn't know it. Remembering this during my healing process now brings me a sense of peace—that somehow, someway, I am still covered by love and prayer.

* * *

In July 2020, a month after the funeral, I flew back to Omaha with 6 family members by my side. We had masks, face shields, and all the protective gear that had become protocol during the pandemic. Only four other adults and the flight crew were on the plane with us. It was as close to a private jet as I will ever be. I was happy to have my family by my side. They were taking a risk flying at all, and they did it for me.

My daughter, Ginger, and her boys, Kam, Kris, and Kai stayed a couple of weeks and my two oldest grandchildren, Staesha and Jaylen stayed the summer. We accomplished a lot. We rearranged the main bedroom, and packed and moved some of Mac's things to the basement.

After I dropped the teens off at the airport, I returned home alone. My home seemed bigger than ever. I closed some of the doors and chose to never venture into most of the house. I slept on the very edge of the king-sized bed that we once shared.

Reflections

When you attended the service of your loved one, how did you feel?
What are some of the memories of your loved one's service?
What stands out for you?
What would your loved one feel about the service?

Do you have a village that supported you and your family during your time of grief? Are you a part of a village that supports others?

Tell your story – it matters.

If you need more room to write, I invite you to continue in your journal

Chapter 6

Whispers In The Night

"No one ever told me that grief felt so like fear."
– C.S Lewis

People say that nothing good happens during the late hours of the night. Whether it's a simple cold, the worst crime, or a wave of grief.

Three months after Mac transitioned, I was lying on the edge of my bed. It was another sleepless night, about 2 or 3 am. I was scrolling through my phone to find someone to call. I just wanted to talk to someone. Looking at name after name, I would reason in my mind why I couldn't dial that number. "They have to go to work", "They don't have the time", "I can't wake her out of her sleep". On and on, this kind of self-talk kept popping into my mind. I didn't feel at ease to call anyone that night – my daughter, sons, sister, brother, cousin or friend.

With hundreds of names in my phone and on Facebook, I felt like I had no one.

Mac's prophetic words from the night before he passed came to mind. "You know what Gwen, we are on our last leg. And we don't have anyone to take care of us." I traveled back in time to that moment and pictured him sitting at the dining table as I sat on the sofa.

In this moment, lying in bed all alone, his words rang true.

Perhaps he knew his time to depart this world had come. It was as if he knew we would not have each other soon. We took care of each other. He had my back and I had his. Those words added a depth and gravity to that moment as I laid in bed, not having anyone to readily call that night.

* * *

A few nights later – another one of many sleepless nights – I called my neighbor, Polly. She had specifically told me to call her at any time and I believed her offer was genuine. The ringing of the phone woke her from her sleep, but she answered and we talked for a while and said good morning. Thank God I felt comfortable making the phone call; and thank God for Polly, my Omaha neighbor. She is a divine connection, God placed her in my life for a reason and a season.

For months, I had nightmares and sleepless nights. At one of my lowest points, on a September Monday morning, I woke up tired and exhausted. I had a horrible night. I slept in the chair downstairs because the previous night I had nightmares. I felt like I had been wrestling with demon spirits. I say this, knowing that I wrestled with something.

There had been an earthquake in California. I had chatted with Dorothy downstairs. We chatted and I fell asleep. I woke up out of one of those nightmares, where I'm pinned down by a force and cannot move or scream. I broke loose, screamed and called my sister but I didn't tell her what happened. It was real, but strange and somewhat unbelievable, so I thought it best to keep it to myself. We hung up, I went to sleep and the same thing happened again.

It was horrible, horrible, horrible. This time, it happened at about 4 am. I was wide awake, struggling, wrestling, trying to scream, something was holding me down, pressing on my body and mugging my mouth. I was kicking and finally I could scream but no one could hear me, I was the only one in the house.

It was gone and I was drained, but no one was there and no one knew but me. I scrolled through my phone desperately searching for someone to call or text and there was no one. I stayed up until daylight, then I went to bed and slept until 11 am.

I was exhausted. It was hard to believe, but it was all true, so real. Could I be wrestling with a demon?

This has happened several times over the past years. I have shared with only a few people and only a handful of people have described the same type of thing happening to them. It was horrible. I stayed home all day and had told my sister I would come over to visit but I decided not to go. Yes, I wanted to be around others but I also wanted to rest, I went to Chick-fil-a, got some fries and came back home. I wanted to tell my sister, and when I started to tell her of my experience, I felt as if I was having a panic attack.

I couldn't get the words out of my mouth. She wouldn't understand.

My blood pressure had been extremely high that day, I was exhausted, washed out. I was afraid for my health and imagined all sorts of things. Eventually, I checked my BP again and it had gone down. I decided I would sleep downstairs in a chair, with an ottoman, with the lights on. I was restless. I slept on and off uncomfortably through the night, but this time, without a nightmare or attack.

Early in the morning, I texted my dear angel friend and told her of my restless night and she said she would come over the next day.

* * *

I was excited that my friend was coming over. I grabbed Mac's John Deere hat, and took the John Deere mower out the garage and mowed the lawn. Mowing the lawn always makes me feel close to Mac. It's funny how I never mowed the grounds when he was alive. That was his toy and nobody else was allowed to play with it. But since he's gone, I have learned to drive it, just like I have learned to do so many other things that I had never done before.

This was the first time I had a friend come over since the pandemic. She was coming at 2 pm. I was so excited that I was going to have a face to face visit with a friend, she had become a dear friend. I waited in the garden, with our chairs socially distanced apart. She came bearing thoughtful gifts – a plaque with "Thankful Thessalonians 5:18", and a journal. It is in this journal that I recorded most of my memories. This afternoon was like a refreshing cold glass of water in the desert. After the deep conversations with her, I was encouraged. I fell asleep in my chair but when I woke up, I started to color in my coloring book.

I had been reminded in my bible study Table Talk group to read and meditate on Proverbs 3:24 "When you lie down, you will not be afraid; Yes, you will lie down and your sleep will be sweet". I slept with my bible open across my chest opened to Proverbs 3:24 and had a wonderful sweet sleep.

*　*　*

Once during the first year, I was in bed and I heard a voice that said "Hey". I had woken up about 20 minutes earlier and looked at the clock. 6 am. I laid back down and as clear as day, I heard the "Hey". I was not sure who it sounded like.

I thought it was my late mother, whom I lovingly call Muhdea. Then I thought it might have been my sister Dorothy. I don't know. I'm not sure but I was shaken. It was not scary or threatening; it felt calming, like someone was looking out for me and wanted me to know something.

I laid there for a while, absorbing the moment, but then I got up and kept putting one foot in front of the other, walking right into my day. This happened on May 3, 2021.

At the time, I found it unusual and mysterious. It was a personal encounter I kept to myself until now. It was unacknowledged, yet undeniably real.

Looking back, I wonder if this was an answer to my silent prayers, in those dark moments, when grief and fear seemed overwhelming. This gentle voice might have been a reminder that I wasn't truly alone.

The mysteries of life and death, the voices we hear, and the solace we find in unexpected places remind me that even in our darkest times, we can find glimpses of hope and comfort. Life, after all, continues to offer us signs of love and presence, even in the most profound moments of sorrow.

Reflections

Some of the incidents I experienced during my first year of grieving were so bizarre and mysterious. In addition to the ones I've already shared, there were countless other strange occurrences that kept me awake and restless.

But today, I thank God that I've made it through that difficult season. I sleep well now, and I am deeply grateful for the peace of a good night's rest.

If you're struggling with disturbed sleep, I want to encourage you—keep going, keep trying to find rest. Take care of yourself and prioritize your health. Know that better days are coming, even when it feels like they won't.

What is keeping you up at night?

What have you been holding inside, unspoken?

Tell your story – it matters.

If you need more room to write, I invite you to continue in your journal

Chapter 7

Strength In The Storm

"Courage doesn't always roar. Sometimes, courage is the little voice at the end of the day saying 'I'll try again tomorrow'."

– Mary Anne Radmacher

Omaha was expecting the first snow of the season. It was Saturday, about 38 degrees, and I knew anything below 35 was considered freezing. The weatherman said it would freeze that night. I got dressed, went out into the cold and scurried around to finish 'winterizing' the house. I had to get snow salt from Walmart and get back by 3pm to get the yard items stored away and set for the snow.

I realized just how much Mac carried and how the two of us had been greater than one. It was a time of adjusting to secondary losses and everything fell on me. It was exhausting.

As I was completing some of the tasks around my house, my neighbor came out. He said "There's a storm coming", and I replied "I know she's coming." He talked about how bad it was going to be, how he's not a homeowner but it looked like he was all set. He said "God Bless you" and went into the house.

He saw me working around the yard but didn't ask if he could help with anything. I would have likely taken him up on the imaginary offer, but just the fact that he said "God Bless You" and didn't offer any help... what?

I continued to finish my tasks for the day. One of the trickiest, most time-consuming tasks was to get the truck, car, riding lawn mower, and snow blower all situated into the garage. Once everything was inside, it had to be snuggled in properly so that the door closed. This was something that Mac and I did together. I never really had to worry about it.

I proceeded to drive the mower out of the garage. I parked it in the driveway, just fine, then put some gas in the tank and restarted the mower. But smoke started bellowing out the engine area. I cut the engine off, restarted it, and the same thing happened. Again and again. I let it cool off, tried again, but couldn't get it to start. I was exhausted and frustrated.

My brother-in-law and my brother were both out of town. Here I am stuck with no one to help me. I thought briefly about what Mac had said the night before he passed, "We are on our last leg and we have no one to help us".

I called another neighbor and told him what happened, to which he said "I'm not home." But then he proceeded to question me "Did you put gas in the right place?" I felt he was talking down to me. I couldn't take it. I became teary-eyed and said "sorry to bother you", he said "no bother".

I wanted to just scream and cry.

I tried to remain strong, sucking it up and trying to hold back the tears, but soon the tears were flowing uncontrollably, I was angry, mad, and sad at the same time. With my adrenaline flowing, I used all my strength to push, then stop, push and stop till I ended up pushing this damn 435-pound mower for 25 feet, all the way to the garage!

While pushing, all I could think of was my encounter with my next door neighbor earlier. He had watched me struggle, but walked away, saying "God Bless you".

As I thought of this interaction, pushing the riding mower into the garage, I was sniffling and holding back my tears. Now I ask myself – why didn't I just have a boo hoo temper tantrum and fall out on the cold ground, kick and scream? That's what I felt like doing, and maybe, just maybe somebody would help me. But I continued to work, collected the last of the flower pots and patio chairs from the yard, and secured them on the patio under the blue tarp.

I went over to the garbage cans, opened the lid and looked in. There was a family of mice at the bottom of the can. I quickly closed the top down tight and shook my head. What should I do? I just wanted to scream at the top of my lungs. No one to call.

Oh I miss my husband.

I took a deep breath and resolved to finish up the outside chores. It took a while, but I got the truck, Mercedes, and tractor mower situated in the garage. Somehow, I managed to close the garage door. It was a very tight squeeze, but I did it.

And I did it all by myself.

At this point, I was crying, tired, and my arms were bruised black and blue.

I had a glass of wine, took a hot bath and tried to relax. I realized that I'm a very strong woman. Without any help, I pushed a John Deere mower tractor into the garage, faced a family of mice, cleaned the yard, felt like I was talked down to by one neighbor and instead of help, I received a God Bless you from another. I did what I had to do.

* * *

A few days later, I thought of the mice in the trash can situation and went out to deal with it. They were still there, but dead. I had to remove them, put them in a bag, and wash out the trash cans. I put ammonia in each. It was a nasty dirty disgusting job but what was I going to do? I had a self-talk moment and said to myself, "you do what you got to do and keep on stepping".

If I don't do it, who will? So I did away with the stinky ugly mice, threw pellets around the house to hopefully detour and keep the mice out. Then my neighbors pulled into their driveway and we waved, and I kept going. All I can remember is him saying "God Bless you" and not offering a helping hand.

On that day, I felt like everyone has their own issues to deal with, so I felt I would keep mine to myself. Everything that needed to be done, got done that day.

I went inside and reflected on the day – the tasks accomplished, the variety of emotions I experienced, and the bruises I gathered. I was feeling like a winner! I browsed SW airline and an ad grabbed my attention, reading "from Omaha to winter warmth."

I purchased a ticket and left behind the weight of winter.

* * *

Our home backs up to the woods, and beyond the woods is a beautiful lake. During the winter, it is common for mice to seek warmth inside the house. This winter was no different. I had seen droppings here and there. My brother-in-law, Paul, showed me how to set up mice traps. He had to show me over and over and over again, since I had never set a mouse trap before. I laid out the traps one night and found three mice had been caught in them the next morning. What now?

I had a conversation with myself.

Self-talk moments had become a part of my new normal. It went like this – "Gwen you do what you have to do, there is no one to physically pick them up but you right?" "Yep!" So I did what I had to do. I swept them onto the dust pan, put them in a trash bag and threw them outside the front door, onto the bench into the freezing cold snow. I would deal with that later.

My blood pressure seemed to be okay now. I was proud of myself, brave and courageous. Exhausted and stressed, hating every minute of disposing of the mice, but I felt I could do anything now.

It was an Alicia Keys, "Superwoman" moment. I thought of the words of her song.

Cause I am a Superwoman,
Yes I am (Yes, she is)

Still when I'm a mess
I still put on a vest With a "S" on my chest
Oh yes, I'm a Superwoman (Yes, she is)
Oh, let me tell you, I am Superwoman, yes, I am (Yes she is)

I could identify with this in part. I sent my sister, Stephanie, a text about feeling like a superwoman doing this, but I was exhausted and stressed and didn't want to be a superwoman.

She replied "You are a real trooper".

I wore this as a badge of honor, "I'm a real trooper."

Reflections

We know that life is not always peaches and cream; a lot of the time the road is rocky. The battles are real, the stress is real, your emotions are real.

What are some of the day-to-day practicalities that are now challenging without your loved one around? What responsibilities did they carry in your life that you have no choice but to take on?

How has that journey been for you?

Tell your story – it matters.

If you need more room to write, I invite you to continue in your journal

Chapter 8

Divinely Connected Community

"Too often, we underestimate the power of
a touch,
a smile,
a kind word,
a listening ear,
an honest compliment,
or the smallest act of caring,
all of which have the potential to turn a life around".

– Leo Buscaglia

God Connects the dots of the Heart and it leads to the next steps.

There's so much I can understand now that I couldn't see in the past. At the very start of my grief journey, God sent people (I call them angels) into my life to minister to me. He continues to send people into my life, some to say hello and cheer my day; others for a season and they step away and others for most of my lifetime. Each person in my community is there for a reason, and most of the time it is in hindsight that I understand the reason.

I now see how God strategically placed them there to walk with me – up and down and through the pathways of grief.

Once I returned to Omaha, I also started to return to a few of the joys and routines that I experienced when Mac was here with me. Going for morning walks, watering the lawn, tending to my flower garden, and attending gatherings (via Zoom).

One morning, after a walk, I stopped, sat in the garden, and texted a dear friend. "I love how the Lord is leading, calling, and ushering me into a new, unfamiliar normal, as I put one foot in front of the other, trusting Him. I thank Him for loving me. I thank Him for sending you into my life, at a time like this. He foresaw this day coming when we first met; and I thank you for all that you are and do."

This is my friend, Donna, a widow, who has become a great friend since the passing of Mac. She became my mentor. She traveled the same path I am on, two years ahead of me.

I first met Donna in 2018 at my annual Garden Tea Party, almost two years before Mac passed. She was a guest of one of my invited friends, Sister Crockett, who was also my bible study teacher. Donna met Mac there too. I later found out that this was Donna's first outing since the passing of her husband a few months earlier. I am a very visual person, and for me, she was the vision of a woman who had experienced loss. She was thriving as she walked in restoration. She had walked in my shoes, and when she spoke, I was reassured that I would be okay. Her unspoken understanding and empathy are a true gift of God to me.

When I ventured into thoughts of tomorrow, I would quickly find myself overwhelmed, stopped in my tracks being pulled under with the quicksands of grief. Since my return to Omaha, Donna continually encouraged me to keep putting one foot before the other and this is exactly what I did. She helped me lean into my loss and grief, what that meant and how that looked. She understood me and what I was going through like no one else.

She once told me, "God had crossed our paths for a reason and to rely on His wisdom. Just put one foot in front of the other and do what you need to do." There were times when I felt like I should be further ahead, or *over it*. She reminded me, "You are still a babe in your new normal". I heard what she said and it helped me refocus and see myself in that light and it was okay to grieve. Her sage advice helped me while I gathered the strength to pick up each foot and move forward. Often, when I least expected it, yet most needed it, **my angel friend would call, saying she cooked dinner, fried fish, freshly** baked bread, peach cobbler, she even once made lavender ice cream and she would drop it off to me around 3 pm.

What a blessing – she thought of me when making her dinner! I was hungry, but didn't feel like cooking or going out, this made me smile. God knew what I needed, she had walked in my shoes and she knew my sorrows in missing my husband, what my grief journey looked like and she prayed for me and did the most thoughtful things. I will forever call Donna, my angel friend, God knew exactly what He was doing when He connected the dots of our lives.

* * *

Around the fourth month, I found one of my greatest joys during the pandemic was interacting with my Zoom community. I woke up excited for the first day of my new bible study group, Bible Study Fellowship (BSF). I got up early and went for a morning walk, listening to scripture and looking around taking in all of God's creation – the green trees, the birds chirping, the blue sky, the gigantic white clouds, everything was beautiful.

As I walked, I had a conversation with God and asked Him "Show me what it means to follow You today." Later, God led me to sit in bible study and He graciously placed a teacher, Linda, in my life. In her intro, she said, "*I'm a widow*", my ears perked up and I listened closely. She had been married to her husband for 21 years and then she said something that rested with me, *"God had other work for me to do and I'm not sure I could have done it if my husband was here"*.

This, in a distant way, resonated with me. I kept this in the back of my mind and wondered if there was truth in this for me. I went on to introduce myself to the group saying, "I'm a new widow, lived in Omaha for 10 years and most of my family is in California." I talked about my love for God's word, morning walks, gardening, nature, and traveling. I felt comfortable, welcomed, and at home in this group. After bible study, I felt really good. The peace of God reigned with me. I grabbed Mac's Clippers cap, (the Clippers was his all-time favorite basketball team) took the John Deer riding mower out of the garage, and mowed the yard. This always made me feel close and connected to Mac.

Linda called me the next day and every week thereafter with words of encouragement. We had deep conversations about the road ahead without my husband. I remember clearly when she told me "Don't let anyone tell you how to grieve." She would say "give yourself time to grieve, it may take you years to accept it all".

I took this sage advice to heart. Linda was in my life for a season of less than a year. I am no longer in contact with Linda but I thank God for her and how she was planted in my life as one widow to help another.

I traveled back and forth between Omaha and Long Beach. It had been five months when I returned to California for a few weeks. I visited the cemetery often, still having moments of disbelief that he was not coming back home.

Meanwhile, God continued to place people in my path, in the oddest of places.

I found myself going to the cemetary 3-4 times a week. It was as though my car was on autopilot. I still can't believe Peewee is there, under the ground. Sometimes I would take flowers and other times I would just take my watering container to water the grass.

I have met many nice widows there; we all lost our husbands in 2020 during the pandemic and we shared stories and exchanged phone numbers. It's almost like a widow's club – me, Gloria and Martha.

"I love and miss my husband." I said in a conversation with lifelong friend, Sister Ford, and the widow of my long-time pastor, Pastor Ford. Pastor Ford had married me and Mac. She was at my wedding, and now nearly 44 years later, she was there for me at his graveside services.

I recall she whispered to me at the services, 'Would you like a bottle of water?', I looked up to receive it and nodded my head. It was as though she offered me a cup of hope, an assurance that I would make it through this day and it was going to be alright. My heart smiled through all the sadness. Although she did not say anything, some messages are conveyed without words.

Months later, she said to me, "it will get better with time." I received this sage advice, even though I didn't know what it meant then. It's only now that I am starting to grasp its meaning.

For now, it means that it won't be a magical line that I would simply cross over and be okay. It's that the waves of grief will not be as intense. A gradual peace of mind, an acceptance of reality, and adjustments to a new complex normal will happen. Its meaning is evolving, but for right now, it is not associated with "moving on" but "moving forward" – with special forever memories.

Mac is not here but I carry him every day in my heart.

***

Next spring, during the pandemic, Joan came over to visit. I first met Joan a couple of years before Mac's passing at Wenninghoff's Farmer market in Omaha. I had on a T-shirt that read, "In this world, not of it, Romans 12:2". She approached me, saying how she liked my shirt and that scripture, and a conversation ensued. We exchanged phone numbers, had lunch a few times and talked often about the

Lord. She also attended one of my Write Your Vision, Make It Plain Workshops and we bonded as true sisters in Christ.

When she learned of Mac's death, she sent me an email, which included a song she had written, recorded and sung for me, titled "Hold Me". I still listen to that song sometimes. It brings me comfort.

One day, Joan and I sat in my beautiful flower garden, she brought me a small vase of lavender flowers from what she called her "quiet space garden". She wrote me a song, and sang it. It was lovely. She asked how I was doing. I told her I was "Better. going through the motions."

I told her of my restless nights and nightmares, but I don't think she quite got it. She couldn't relate, and I wasn't going into details. What if she thought I was crazy?

We segued into another subject and enjoyed our time together. Joan was in my life for a beautiful season and I thank the Lord for comforting me and wiping my tears with her presence. Although Joan and I are no longer in regular contact, she was most assuredly an angel planted in my life for a reason and a season.

Each week, I look forward to the Tuesday morning Bible study, it was a small group of 5 ladies, Sister Crocket, Sister Lena, Sister Carol, Sister Clarease and myself, where the connections and conversations were real. We are surrounded by God's love, uplifting and encouraging each other as we study the books of the bible. We had met in person for many years and now, during the pandemic, we made sure we never missed our time together.

I recall being at a Zoom meeting with them a month or so after Mac's burial. I was ambushed by grief. I leaned into it, and in the middle of a sentence, I found I just couldn't say another word. I started to weep, cry, in the meeting and lean on their virtual shoulders. They covered me, and prayed for me. They were present. I felt safe, felt their love and God's love surround me and console me. I was comforted. We continue our bible study weekly. I thank God for this connection.

* * *

My dear lifelong friend Rosalind, we attended the same church for many years in California but we hadn't talked in several years. But whenever we spoke, it was like we never missed a beat. Do you have friends like that?

She had left me messages of condolences and checked in on me via text. But one day, a few months after Mac passed, the phone rang. It was Rosalind, calling from California, where she lived. We picked up right where we left off, as if we had been talking every day. She said she wanted to come and spend some time with me. I thought she was joking!

The next week, she came to Omaha and spent a week with me. We had so much fun, laughing and talking, taking photos and reminiscing. God knows what you need and when you need it.

* * *

Sunday dinners at my sister Stephanie's I had a standing invite to be a part of the family, and I often took advantage of it. My sister is a great and creative cook — you name it, she can do it. I often had special requests and she made it happen.

My first outing was a summer holiday and I made a banana pudding and potato salad. I was excited to go meet up with my family. I pulled up in the truck and Paul, my brother-in-law, my niece Jamila, her boys, Jamir and Jordyn and Stephanie were in the front yard.

I slowly parked the truck, got out, and the boys met me with hugs and grabbed the dishes. As I was walking, I was ambushed by grief.

I felt so alone.

I reached the steps, sat on the bench, and started to sob; I just melted. It was a real moment of realization — Peewee was not here, and life was going on. He had always been there; I couldn't help it. My niece came and wrapped her arms around me and I sobbed. I could hear her saying, "it's going to be alright, Aunt Gwen." Yes, I know it will. After a while, there was laughter and good eating and I left to go home alone.

My sister, Dorothy, never failed to call me every night, like clockwork. She was a constant that I could count on. Her companion, Mr. D had passed one week before Mac passed, and she was grieving too. I know I had not been there for her. I was not there for myself either. I wanted to go to his services but I couldn't. It's all a blur. I truly was going through the motions.

For the first year, my nephew, Derrick, texted me every single morning to say good morning and wish me a good day. Derrick's father, Cardell, and Mac, were brothers. Cardell passed 7 months before Mac. And Mac's other brother, Wardell passed 10 months after Mac. It is surreal that the three brothers passed away within an 18-month period.

All this was during the pandemic, there was lots of loss in my family, in my community, in the world. The life that we once knew, was no more. It all happened in what seems like a blink of an eye.

About 6 months after Mac's passing, my nephew Rossi sent me a video message expressing his love. He sang me a song to cheer me up. It was right on time, I needed to hear this, my heart smiled. These are the lyrics:

I been thinking of you,

Thinking of you,
Although we are far apart,
You will always be in my heart,
There you will always stay,
Until we meet again someday
I'll be thinking of you
I'll be praying for you, I'll be praying for you
All of your hopes and your dreams
I pray they will come true,
And, should there be some rain,
I know it will shine again,
Cause I'll be praying for you

I replied thanking him for thinking of me. "Your song and prayer are right on time. I needed that more than you will ever know. I love you dearly" with tears escaping my eyes and streaming down my cheeks.

* * *

In Omaha, about nine months after Peewee passed, the quicksand of grief was heavy. I was finding this to be a lonely season of life. I prayed for an outlet to vent my feelings.

I would sit in my office and research online resources, I was looking for support groups and heard about GriefShare. There were a lot of churches offering this support, but for the longest time, I didn't reach out to gather more information.

For some reason, I wasn't comfortable in many ways with showing up on what I felt would be a cold call with strangers. I didn't want to pretend in any manner; I didn't want to feel like I had to be fake. I didn't have the energy and for a long time I decided I wasn't up to trying to fit in, and all that.

So I continued to pray and kept looking. I said to a friend, "I know God will answer because I'm finding this to be a lonely season of life."

Shortly after that, I located the GriefShare support group, in California, and met Angel and Linda, the group leader. Truly divine connections. Angel, Linda and GriefShare are angels God sent into my life in a tender season, to minister healing. I am still in contact with them today.

The Lord directed me to them. For a season, I would find myself there each Monday in the zoom meeting. Although it was with a group of strangers, it felt like kin/family. We had so much in common, the loss of a loved one and the understanding that comes along with the grieving. It was a special place where I found a community in my loss.

The GriefShare book, Loss Of A Spouse says it beautifully: "At GriefShare, the people there truly get it. They know the emotions, the exhaustion, the struggle just to function. They don't rush or judge another person in grief, because they understand that each person's grief is unique".

I found it to be just what I needed; I could open up and they truly understood the full gamut of grief.

It was a group of maybe 10 to 15 of us, from all over the United States and each one in the group had suffered the loss of a loved one. Angel, her son and Linda, her daughter; Madison, his wife; Janet her husband, and many, many others. We all had a story. There was no pretense. You could speak or not; you could listen or not; you could share your experience or not. We shared and expressed raw, painful emotions with openness and transparency.

It was like having a warm blanket wrapped around me filled with understanding and comfort, shielding me and providing a refreshing morsel of bread to warm the soul. We were on the same page, even when there were no words on the page. We understood each others' hearts.

During one of the meetings, around the 10th week of the 13-week series, we were given the opportunity to share picture(s) and talk about our loved ones. I chose to share a picture of Mac on his John Deere Mower. My son and daughter had gifted this toy to him for his birthday and he loved it, he would mow the yard proudly. It was his toy and he didn't allow anyone to touch it (not even me!)

He loved it. But now, after a few lessons from my brother-in-law, I got the hang of it pretty quick and have been proudly cutting the yard.

The group was genuinely a place to listen and share. I told them how he was the life of the party. How he loved to tell jokes over and over again and although I'd heard them all a million times, I would still smile each time and shake my head.

At that moment, I tried to think of one of Mac's jokes, and I couldn't remember any of them. And I began to tear up. Why can't I remember? It is so unfair. Why can't I at least have this memory to carry with me? My brain was such a fog relating to this. I have since learned that there is such a thing as brain fog, characterized by confusion, forgetfulness and a lack of focus and mental clarity. And that it is very real and a natural part of grief and directly related to grief.

Then it came to memory in parts about the "Laughing Barrel Mississippi" joke and I asked Stephanie and Paul to fill in the blanks. I hoped they would help me remember. I asked them and they only remembered parts of it but not the details. I still can't quote any of his jokes and this makes me sad. I can visualize him saying the joke, his gestures, his laughing out loud that it was infectious and caused others to laugh and that part makes me smile. And when I hear others telling stories about Mac, I feel how he affected their life and love that we are keeping his memory alive.

***

While in this GriefShare group, I met another widow, Janet, in the southern California area, who lost her husband two months before me. She reached out to me, and since we now live in the same area, we began to take morning walks on the beach and nature walks. We are like-minded sisters in Christ and are now dear friends. God is good.

Over 2 years, I attended three of their 13-week virtual sessions in the GriefShare program. Also I attended two six-week virtual sessions with a Grief group facilitated by Evelyn and Sheila at their Church in Omaha. Evelyn lost her son several years ago and we share the grief journey. In the group sessions, I had the opportunity to share my stories and we shared an unspoken understanding which was exactly what I needed. Evelyn and I are dear friends to this day.

In moments of despair, when grief threatened to pull me under, these connections reminded me that I was never alone. They became the hugs of God's love, reassuring me that even in the most painful times, there is hope and healing. They taught me to lean into my grief, to accept the waves of sorrow as part of the journey, and to trust that, in time, peace would find its way back into my life.

The path of grief is not one we walk alone. It is a journey marked by the love, support, and divine guidance of the angels God sends our way. And for that, I am forever grateful. As I continue to put one foot in front of the other, I know that with every step, I am not only moving forward, but also honoring the memory of Mac, carrying his love with me into the future.

Reflections

As I reflect on the past months, I see how God has gently connected the dots of my heart, leading me to each new step. Every person He placed in my path, from Donna's steadfast support to the shared solace of the GriefShare community, was a lifeline. Each one, whether present for a season or still walking with me, has been an angel on my journey, guiding me through the darkest valleys and lifting me toward the light.

Who are the divine connections in your life? Who has been there for you, whether it's been for a lifetime, for months, a day, or simply passing through the night. Who was sent into your life for a specific reason? Something that you know was not by coincidence – they gave you a message and you now see it as a message from God?

Where and how do you vent your loss or share your grief?

Tell your story – it matters.

_____

_____

If you need more room to write, I invite you to continue in your journal

Chapter 9

Dancing With Memories

"What the heart has once known, it shall never forget".
– Author unknown

One day, I was in the garage, where Mac spent a lot of time. It was his man cave, where he loved playing music and enjoying himself simply watching the cars passing by.

We lived in the suburbs, where there was little activity. Not too many children playing or traffic passing by. With the bipolar weather in Omaha, most people stayed indoors most of the time. Mac used to watch the cars and wave to neighbors passing by in cars or on foot.

This is reminiscent of the South – a part of Southern hospitality. Mac was from Alabama and it was part of his personality to speak to people, even if they did not speak or wave and say hello to everyone. He brought his Southern hospitality to the midwest suburbs and he knew almost everyone in the neighborhood by simply waving and making himself friendly. He could strike up a conversation with anyone.

As I was sitting in the garage in his chair, reflecting and thinking about our times together, I played one of his favorite Johnny Taylor CDs. I turned the volume up on one of the songs, "*I Believe In You (You Believe In Me)*" just as he would do. He would open the kitchen screen door as I was cooking or in the middle of doing something and he would say, "Come dance with me, come sit and let's talk". Most of the time, I was too busy. I thought I would have this forever and I rarely stopped what I was doing to join him.

Now I know how important such moments are, and how they shouldn't be taken for granted. Now they are a memory.

I envisioned him snapping his finger, moving his head, reaching out his hand. But he was not there.

Oh how I wish I could dance with my husband again.

Then I changed the music to Luther's song, "Dance With My Father Again", I closed my eyes. I imagined and pictured him saying "Come dance with me, sweetheart" and with tears flowing, I began to dance the cha cha, as if he were there.

On my first wedding anniversary without him, my grandkids, Jaylen and Staesha were visiting me. As I was sitting on my swing in my flower garden when they surprised me with a bunch of gifts, snacks, candy and a picture collage of me and Peewee. How sweet of them! They hugged me and said I love you. I made a live Facebook video that day and still watch it back to cherish how special it was.

*　*　*

As my birthday was approaching, almost three months after he passed, I was in Omaha and missing Peewee terribly. I didn't know what to expect. This was my first birthday without him and definitely was not in a mood to celebrate. My only desire was to get through it. My sister asked what I wanted for my birthday, what I wanted to do and I said crab boil would be nice. It sounded nice at the time and although I accepted my sister's kind invitation to have a special dinner, I really just wanted to stay home alone.

On my birthday, all my Omaha family (my sister, brother in law, brother, niece and grand-nephews) came over to celebrate. They came with boxes and boxes of all the fixins for a grand party, two pans full of Cajun seafood boil. It was loaded with shrimp, crab, andouille, potatoes, eggs, and corn on the cob. I could smell the garlic and it looked delicious, a cake, drinks, decorations. As we were hovering in the kitchen dining area, I was wondering why there was so much food, there were just 7 of us. It was moments later, I experienced my first ever true surprise. One by one, my California family came in through the basement and up the stairs. I can only imagine my face, but I was so happy and surprised beyond my imagination. Ginger, my daughter, Keron, my son-in-law, and Chris, my son, had flown in just for my birthday! Tears of joy and happiness flowed. I really needed that, a true surprise birthday party. We had a fun weekend celebrating my birthday.

***

Later that year, 2020, in the winter months, still in the heart of the pandemic I was missing community and family gatherings. I saw a need for and was led to start up, what I named Granny's Sunday School for my grandkids. Jaylen, Jeff, Amajay, Jr, Staesha and Kameron attended, and the younger ones, Kris, Kai and Abby would come and sit in at the end of the class. It was a basic bible class, a meaningful way to connect with my grandchildren; it gave me joy to meet them on Zoom call every Sunday morning to teach them about God, Jesus and the Bible basics.

Thanksgiving has always been my favorite holiday, filled with cherished memories of large family gatherings at my homes in California and Omaha. But this year was different—it was my first Thanksgiving without him. I returned to California for dinner with my daughter and her family. I got up early to make a couple of dishes, cornbread dressing and banana pudding, and then drove alone to her house.

Everything was festive, and the family was all there. But at the dinner table, one seat stood out. My daughter had draped a cover over a chair and made a plaque for her dad. In honoring the empty chair, we honored him, keeping his presence with us, even though he was no longer physically there. It reminded me of President Biden's words, "There are many tables with empty seats where someone once sat." Though his chair was vacant, the love and memories filled the room.

Despite our attempts to follow social distancing rules, we couldn't help but come together. We enjoyed the day, and afterward, we each went to our separate homes, carrying his memory with us.

* * *

My second thanksgiving I spent in Omaha and my son, Jason and his wife, Nicole drove in from Texas for the weekend. It was so good to have a family visit, to have voices and laughter in the house for a few days. On Thanksgiving day, I made potato salad, a ham and my famous banana pudding; we packed it up and went over to have dinner with Stephanie, Paul and the Omaha family. It was a memorable day. My son stayed a couple of more days, helping me sell items and then he packed his car and left.

Reflections

How can you gently navigate the emotional waves and flashbacks that memories may bring?

What are some of the moments, the memories that you cherish, the ones that make your heart smile?

Think of a song that brings your loved one to mind. Was there a special song you shared? Reflect on why this song is meaningful to you. If there are others, consider creating a playlist that you can turn to in moments of loneliness or longing.

Enjoy those moments – whether it's now or then, the now of the moment or in a memory from back then. They are yours, forever to keep, sent and meant to bring you joy.

Tell your story – it matters.

_____

_____

_____

_____

_____

_____

_____

_____

_____

_____

If you need more room to write, I invite you to continue in your journal

Chapter 10

Choosing Life: Embracing The New Normal

> *"If you can't fly run,*
> *If you can't run walk,*
> *If you can't walk then crawl,*
> *But whatever you do,*
> *You have to keep moving forward."*
> *– Rev. Dr. Martin Luther King*

Not a day passes without hearing Peewee's voice echo in my heart. His familiar tone, filled with wit and wisdom, speaks to me constantly, as if he's still here, weighing in on the little moments of life. His words, always present in the background of my thoughts, bring warmth and an unexpected smile, reminding me that while he may be gone, his presence lingers, offering comfort and company in ways only he could.

He encourages me to keep on living.

When I heard Jeanette Winterson say, "I discover that grief means living with someone who is not there," it felt like she had captured the essence of my daily reality. Those words painted a perfect picture of my life without Mac. I've come to know and accept that he is gone, but his imprint lingers in the fabric of my thoughts and actions, shaping how I navigate each day.

I have come to realize that there will always be waves of grief associated with the loss of my husband, some waves will bring high tides and upsurges of grief. They will come and go. As I track past the fourth year, there are certain days or weeks that bring with them a season of depression, a surge of anxiety or an emotional unbalance. I am adjusting. I know that this is a part of my new normal.

I know significant dates and times of the year trigger deep grief for me, they include our wedding date, his birthdate, my birthday, the day of his passing, the day of his funeral, Valentine's Day, Thanksgiving, Christmas. And other times, it's a certain smell, or seeing a couple in the grocery store, or simply that I hear Johnny Taylor, Luther Vandross, or Whitney Houston's ballad I'll Always Love You.

I can be blindsided by a tsunami of grief.

I have never just sat still very well, and for the past four years, I have kept myself extremely busy. Almost every waking hour is filled with busy-ness. I realize it has been a good cover-up. It has helped mask the effects of being alone, but the emotions surfaced at some point anyhow. I am exhausted now and one way or another, they must have a place to vent.

Tyler Perry hit the nail on the head in a powerful message: "Grief is a very living thing, it visits at random. I tried to work it away, I tried to drink it away, I booked myself like crazy and all it did was wait for me to finish. So when it shows up, however it shows up, let it show up."

I've deliberately avoided gatherings that bring couples and marriage to the forefront of my mind, but recently, it happened unexpectedly. I went to my first party surrounded by married couples, and as soon as I walked in and greeted the hosts, I felt a wave of discomfort and awkwardness wash over me. It was overwhelming—my instinct was to escape, to run home and shield myself from the pain of missing Mac. But instead, I stepped outside to breathe, trying to steady myself. There, I found a young woman standing alone, and we struck up a conversation. Little by little, the heavy weight of grief began to lift, and I eventually found the strength to rejoin the gathering. In the end, to my surprise, the evening was filled with laughter—something I hadn't expected when I first walked through that door.

I have found that key dates carry with them a high likelihood of giving me an anxiety attack, or leading me into a state of depression, or a stress-related migraine. They can be turbulent hurricanes of emotions. During these times, I have found that I fare best if I plan ahead and enter into the storm with intention and purpose. Sometimes it's best for me to travel and get away from my day-to-day, to do something special. I like to take my mind off of the day by doing something different or adventuresome.

During a conversation with my friend Evelyn recently, I identified a certain trait in myself – I am a runner. I run away from the familiar, to a new and different adventure. That is how I have chosen to deal with it so far.

In months of May and June, I plan a solo getaway to reflect. I make it a real adventure – going to a new place and doing something different. I explore places alone, but I take the best memories of Mac with me wherever I go.

Around the first anniversary, in 2021, I went on a road trip to downtown Chicago, where I had reservations on the Magnificent Mile. Every day, I walked around exploring the city. On the day of Mac's heart attack, I made reservations for one at the Grand Lux cafe and enjoyed chicken Jambalaya for dinner. I took my time and reflected on all that happened a year prior when Mac had his heart attack. On other days, I enjoyed the architectural cruise tour. I had a wonderful solo time; then off to California, then to Dallas, going to the pool with my son. I actually put on a swim suit and got in the water.

On the second anniversary, I jetted off to Honolulu Hawaii. I went to Waikiki Beach where I rested, walked, and for the first time ever, joined a congregation for church services on the beach. I walked over 20 miles during my week-long stay on the island. Mac and I had been to this same island, Oahu, in 2006 for our 30th Anniversary and had an unforgettable time. It was most memorable. There was a 6.7 magnitude earthquake and tsunami warning. Nothing like that happened this time, just the time of my life.

On the third anniversary, I took a solo road trip with the memory of my soul mate. I drove a couple of hours to the inland valley, the wine country of Temecula, California. I spent my time at a luxurious bed and breakfast suite that opened up to the view of the sprawling vineyards, enjoying time alone, horseback riding, sightseeing and checking out the wineries.

On the fourth anniversary, I took a **50-mile boat ride and sped across the ocean to Catalina Island for a few days.**

My solo adventures have become a metaphor for my ongoing journey with grief. Each trip has been a way to honor Mac's memory while also carving out space for my own growth and healing. From the bustling streets of Chicago to the tranquil beaches of Honolulu, these experiences have offered moments of reflection and renewal.

* * *

My family and I have designated the first Saturday of June as a day to remember Mac. This annual event is aptly named "Wear a Hat for Mac" Day, where family and friends gather to celebrate his life. He had a collection of hats and caps that he loved to wear. You rarely saw him without sporting one. The family and friends would pick a hat or cap from Mac's collections and wear it throughout the day.

The annual "Wear a Hat for Mac" Day has become a cherished tradition, a testament to the love and laughter we continue to hold dear. The hats, once a symbol of Mac's everyday charm, now serve as a vibrant reminder of his presence in our lives. We laugh, we share stories, and we celebrate the essence of who he was to each of us - Mac, Peewee, Dad, Pops, pawpaw. We find great comfort in the joy he brought to us.

"Don't make rash decisions in the early stages of grief," my Omaha pastor, Pastor Hart, once told me. Others, including my angel friends, echoed this wisdom. It became a cornerstone for me as I navigated the turbulent waters of loss.

Following this advice, I resisted the urge to make major changes immediately after Mac's passing. Instead, I allowed myself time to grieve and heal, postponing any significant decisions. It wasn't until a year and a half later, when I felt more grounded and less overwhelmed by my grief, that I began to sort through our belongings and make plans for the future.

At the end of 2021, after careful consideration and with a clearer sense of readiness, I sold my beautiful home in Omaha. The moving trucks were loaded with my possessions, and on Christmas Eve of 2021, I boarded a flight to Ontario, California. Arriving there, I was greeted by the warmth of family and the festive spirit of the season. This move marked not just a physical relocation but a symbolic step forward, blending old memories with new beginnings as I celebrated Christmas with those I loved.

Reflections

My inner dialogue never stops, like today: Breathe in, breathe out. Inhale, exhale. Gwen, keep putting one foot in front of the other to keep living. Mac would want you to live again, just as you would want the same for him. It's okay, and he's okay. You've got to live, not only for yourself but for others. Open your eyes of faith and see that your journey isn't over. You haven't reached your destiny yet. There's still more of this abundant life to live, carrying your loved ones with you in your heart.

What are some ways in which you are moving forward on your grief journey with the memories of your loved one? How are you embracing your new normal?

Do you have any new habits or rituals that you've established to honor and remember your loved one?

Tell your story – it matters.

If you need more room to write, I invite you to continue in your journal

Epilogue

As I walk in restoration and continue the healing process, I often find myself longing to turn back the hands of time, to have my husband here with me again. But I know this isn't possible. I've come to accept the finality of his physical absence, and I carry him in my heart. If given the choice to erase our relationship to avoid the heartache, I wouldn't take it. I would endure the pain a thousand times over.

I am profoundly grateful for the years we shared, for our family, and for his salvation. I am thankful for the transformation and the ministry that has been birthed, and the woman I am becoming out of this pain. My life and character were shaped from the age of 22 to 66 – 43 years and 10 months with my husband by my side.

It wasn't always easy; there were challenges and hardships along the way. But it was the journey God gave us, and we walked it together.

And I know, with a deep and abiding faith, that one day I will see him again.

Not long after Mac's passing, God sent two fleeting messengers into my life. Though I no longer have contact with either person, their messages still resonate with me, providing context, comfort, and peace. Here are the two messages:

"What if, just what if, part of your destiny in life was to lead your husband to salvation?"

* * *

"God had other work for you to do, and I'm not sure you could have done it if Mac was still here."

* * *

Though many details since May 24, 2020, remain a blur, when I ask myself what I know for sure, this is what I hold onto:

I know I have been blessed beyond measure in every chapter of my life, including this one.

I know that God has carried me through loss and grief, just as He carries me through my migraine headaches. He has given me the power of recall to remind me of the countless ways He has seen me through. I trust Him completely to guide me through whatever comes next.

I will forever give God the glory for carrying me through the healing process, for the faith and courage He has instilled in me, and for the community of family, friends, and the village that surrounds and supports me.

My destiny is to keep on living, to speak and minister as an Ambassador for Christ, using my journey and personal life experiences as my testimony of the goodness of God through it all.

* * *

Appendix A

Paying It Forward

I'm sharing the most helpful and practical advice that helped me through my grief. I pray that during your grief journey, you may find solace in this sage advice.

* Don't let anyone tell you how to grieve
* Don't make any major decisions in the first year
* Protect your heart and keep putting one foot in front of the other
* During sleepless nights, listen to the Sleepy story app or Calm App
* Get some adult coloring books and pencils and start coloring
* Seek out a therapist and pour out you heart
* Journal and look back months later and see your progress
* Don't isolate yourself
* Volunteer to help others
* Take care of yourself
* Take long walks
* Listen to music
* Find new ways to celebrate
* Consider making travel plans on anniversaries
* Find a support group such as GriefShare
* Pamper yourself
* Pray Continuously

Appendix B

Scriptures

As you grieve the loss of your loved one, cling close to the promises of God, and find comfort, strength and peace in knowing God's Word.

Hebrews 11:1 (NKJV)
Now faith is the substance of things hoped for, the evidence of things not seen.

※

Philippians 4:7 (NKJV)
and the peace of God, which surpasses all understanding, will guard your hearts and minds through Christ Jesus.

※

Psalm 23 (NKJV)
The LORD is my Shepherd;
I shall not want.
He makes me to lie down in green pastures;
He leads me beside the still waters.
He restores my soul
He leads me in the path of righteousness

For His name's sake.

Yea, though I walk through the valley of the shadow of
death,
I will fear no evil;
For You are with me;
Your rod and Your staff, they comfort me.

You prepare a table before me in the presence of my enemies;
You anoint my head with oil;
My cup runs over.

Surely goodness and mercy shall follow me
All the days of my life;
And I will dwell in the house of the LORD
Forever.

Ecclesiastes 3:1-8 (NKJV)

To everything there is a season,
A time for every purpose under heaven:
A time to be born,
A time to die,
A time to plant,
And a time to pluck what is planted;
A time to kill
And a time to heal;

A time to break down,
And a time to build up;
A time to weep,
And a time to laugh;
A time to mourn,
And a time to dance;
A time to cast away stones,
And a time to gather stones;
A time to embrace,
And a time to refrain from embracing;
A time to gain,
And a time to lose;
A time to keep,
And a time to throw away;
A time to tear,
And a time to sew;
A time to keep silence,
And a time to speak;
A time to love,
And a time to hate;
A time of war,
And a time of peace.

Proverbs 3:5-6 (NKJV)

Trust in the LORD with all your heart,
And lean not on your own understanding;

In all your ways acknowledge Him, And He shall direct your paths.

***

Psalm 9:1-2(NKJV)

I will praise You, O LORD, with my whole heart; I will tell of all Your marvelous works. I will be glad and rejoice in You; I will sing praise to Your name,
O Most High.

***

Psalm 147:3 (NKJV)

He heals the brokenhearted And binds up their wounds.

***

Romans 15:13 (NLT)

I pray that God, the source of hope, will fill you completely with joy and peace because you trust in him. Then you will overflow with confident hope through the power of the Holy Spirit.

***

1 Thessalonians 4: 13-18 (NLT)

13 And now, dear brothers and sisters, we want you to know what will happen to the believers who have died so you will not grieve like people who have no hope.

14 For since we believe that Jesus died and was raised to life again, we also believe that when Jesus returns, God will bring back with him the believers who have died.

15 We tell you this directly from the Lord: We who are still living when the Lord returns will not meet him ahead of those who have died.

16 For the Lord himself will come down from heaven with a commanding shout, with the voice of the archangel, and with the trumpet call of God. First, the believers who have died will rise from their graves.
17 Then together with them, we who are still alive and remain on the earth will be caught up in the clouds to meet the Lord in the air. Then we will be with the Lord forever.
18 So encourage each other with these words.

Matthew 24:36-44 (NKJV)

"But of that day and hour no one knows, not even the angels of heaven, but My Father only. But as the days of Noah were, so also will the coming of the Son of Man be. For as in the days before the flood, they were eating and drinking, marrying and giving in marriage, until the day that Noah entered the ark, and did not know until the flood came and took them all away, so also will the coming of the Son of Man be. Then two men will be in the field: one will be taken and the other left. Two women will be grinding at the mill: one will be taken and the other left. Watch therefore, for you do not know what hour your Lord is coming. But know this, that if the master of the house had known what hour the thief would come, he would have watched and not allow his house to be broken into. Therefore you also be ready, for the Son of Man is coming at an hour you do not expect.

Appendix C

Definitions

These definitions are included to provide clarity and insight into the words that often carry deep emotional weight. In navigating loss, understanding the meaning of these terms can offer comfort, help you process your own journey, and remind you that you are not alone.

Grief /noun/ - deep and poignant distress caused by or as if by bereavement.

Mourn /verb/ - feel or show sorrow for the death of (someone), typically by following conventions such as the wearing of black clothes.
- feel regret or sadness about (the loss or disappearance of something).

Faith /noun/ - complete trust or confidence in someone or something.

Process /noun/ - a series of actions or steps taken in order to achieve a particular end

Community /noun/ - a group of people living in the same place or having a particular characteristic in common.

- the condition of sharing or having certain attitudes and interests in common.

Peace /noun/ - freedom from disturbance; tranquility.
- a state or period in which there is no war or a war has ended.

Strength /noun/ - the quality or state of being physically strong.
- the capacity of an object or substance to withstand great force or pressure.

Courage /noun/ - the ability to do something that frightens one; bravery.
- strength in the face of pain or grief.

Bereave /verb/ - to be deprived of a close relation or friend through their death.

Hope /noun/ - grounds for believing that something good may happen.

Journey /noun/ - a long and often difficult process of personal change and development.

All definitions powered by Oxford Languages

In Loving Memory

Cali Ginger Lavender

March 30 2022 – March 30 2022

Jada Marie Johnson

March 17 2009 – September 1 2024

About Gwen

I am a transition life coach, dedicated to helping women navigate life's challenges and transitions with courage, confidence, and clarity. My passion is to encourage and support each woman in owning her unique story, supporting her to move forward – with purpose and without regrets. I have a deep ability to connect with people facing difficulties, as I have often found myself in similar positions, even if not walking the exact same path.

As a young wife and mother, I founded the Mother-to-Mother support group to assist women navigating significant changes involving their children or grandchildren—a group born from my own personal struggles. In later years, I founded Lavender & SAGE (Sisters Aging with Grace and Elegance) Connections, a community designed to support women in creating more fulfilling lives during their personal transitions.

As someone deeply committed to sharing and uplifting others, I have had the privilege of teaching and speaking on topics such as 'Faith and Trust in God,' 'It's Your Time to Live,' 'Your Beautiful Purpose,' 'Letting Go and Moving Forward,' and more." I welcome the opportunity to share these messages with audiences ready for transformation.

I believe that it's no coincidence when our paths cross. I thank God for every connection made, each one a testament to the power of resilience and renewal.

Thank God for letting our paths cross.

Let's stay connected: contact@gwenlavender.com

www.ingramcontent.com/pod-product-compliance
Lightning Source LLC
LaVergne TN
LVHW020931090426
835512LV00020B/3313